CAMBRID...
ODDFELLOW...
FUNNY TAL...

PENNY
PUBLISHING

Compilation copyright ©1997 Penny Publishing Limited
Text copyright © 1997 Richard Breen
Illustration copyright © 1997 Holte
Designer Tom Gordon

FOREWORD

'At Cambridge, the individual withers, and the world is more and more', so wrote Arthur Gray in 1912. This light-hearted book hopefully illustrates that he could not be more wrong by describing, both from the past and the present, the stories of the individuals, eccentric, good and bad, who lived in the older Cambridge colleges and who helped to create their peculiar traditions and their history.

This is a humorous look at Cambridge men throughout the centuries and references to all characters, living or dead, are in no way intended to be malicious - even Oliver Cromwell had a part to play!

'Cambridge lies in an attitude of magnificent repose, and shaking lazy ears stares at her elder sister, and asks what it is all about.'

Charles Kingsley 1819-1875

CONTENTS

GLOSSARY

BULLDOGS

University police who work under the Proctors.

DIVINE

A clergyman.

DONS

All Cambridge University 'teachers' are known unofficially as 'dons'.

FELLOWS

High ranking dons, formally had to be celibate; they may now marry but must retire at 65.

FELLOWS'
COMBINATION ROOM

Their common room.

GYP

Now mostly known as bedmaker, the 'Scout' in Oxford.

HALL

The college refectory.

HEADS OF COLLEGES

The head of each college is the Master except at King's where he is the Provost and at Queens' where he is the President.

LIVING

A church office endowed with fixed revenues.

OXFORD

A university somewhere in the South.

PORTERS	Located at the entrance gate to each college, they know everything and sometimes wear bowler hats.
PROCTORS	Dons in charge of the Bulldogs and in charge of university discipline.
SEND DOWN	To expel a student from the University.
STATUTES	The often strange rules and regulations laid down for each college by its Founder.
STIPEND	Salary paid to a clergyman.
TITHE	The income given voluntarily to the church or clergy or due as a tax to support them.
VICE-CHANCELLOR	The true Head of the University and elected from among the heads of the colleges. The Chancellor has only been a titular Principal since the middle ages.

CLARE COLLEGE

Clare College is the second oldest college in Cambridge and when it was founded by Richard de Badew as University Hall in 1326 it was so poor it only had two chairs, one for the Master and one for a visitor. Lady Elizabeth de Clare, granddaughter of Edward I, who had pots of money and modern ideas, refounded the College as Clare Hall in 1338 for a Master, 19 Fellows and free board and education for 10 poor boys.

The College coat of arms consists of gold tear drops in a black surround which is a mourning band to remind the world that the Founding Lady had buried three husbands before she was 28 - hence her wealth! Clare Hall was renamed Clare College in 1856. Another benefactor was Sir W. Babyington who died in 1455 and left a 'loan' of 100 marks to the College, which loan was to be cancelled if for 15 years since the anniversary of his death, two priests who had to be Fellows had prayed daily for his soul.

It looks as though the popularity of praying at Clare waned over the centuries as in 1870 a petition was signed by 34 students requesting 'The Reverend the Master and the Reverend and learned Fellows to restore to us the privilege of a weekly celebration of the Holy Communion in our College Chapel'. Surely a unique request from students of any time.

With the 16th century came two totally opposite men, the Martyr and the Cad, who both departed the world with memorable last words. First came Hugh Latimer, a Fellow in 1515, a die-hard Protestant who refused to alter his views in troubled times. As Bishop of Worchester, he was burned at the stake in Oxford, by order of Catholic Queen Mary, together with two other Cambridge men, Bishops Cranmer and Ridley. Latimer does not deserve total pity as he had himself assisted and ranted at the burning of others but he died bravely uttering (probably screaming) the following:

'Be of good comfort Master Ridley and play the man. We shall this day light such a candle by God's grace in England, as shall never be put out.'
One can only guess at Master Ridley's comment ...

The three men's fate led the historian Macaulay to write: 'Cambridge had the honour of educating these celebrated Protestant Bishops whom Oxford had the honour of burning.'

Then came Robert Greene, the prolific Elizabethan dramatist with 38 publications to his name by the time of his death in 1592. Known as a University Wit and writer of rogue literature, Greene was very bad to his young wife whom he betrayed, robbed and deserted. As he lay dying in a lowly garret 'young in years but old in iniquity', he wrote to his wife:

'Doll, I charge thee, by the love of our youth and my soule's rest, that thou wilte see this man paid (his host); for if hee and his wife had not succoured me, I had died in the streets.' Alas, history does not reveal what her colourful reply must have been.

In 1638, the College started to build a new court but it had barely begun when the Parliamentarians arrived during the Civil War and removed all the stones and bricks to fortify Cambridge Castle against the Royalists. Oliver Cromwell eventually paid for the stones and the court was finally completed in 1719 but although the buildings took 81 years to complete, they are harmoniously proportioned - not in the opinion of the wit who said that, since they are overlooked by the massive structure of King's Chapel, it looks like 'an elephant waiting to enter its pen' - over which 'pen', students in 1968 suspended a large black spider called Arabella on a web made of more than one mile of string. The two buildings are indeed so close that years ago a Fellow of Clare 'took to haranguing those going to King's Chapel from the windows of his rooms'.

Someone who was keener on people going to chapel was Nicholas Ferrar. He was a Fellow in 1613, became a Member of Parliament and then decided to retire from life into an Anglican religious community he founded for lay people - the first Happy Clappy commune in Britain. Charles I visited it and found it inspiring; Cromwell, true to form, shut it down.

Another eccentric Fellow was William Butler, at Clare in the 17th century. He was also a very successful doctor and physician to James I, with novel ideas for treating his patients. On one occasion he cured a man suffering from an opium overdose by slitting open the belly of a cow and putting the man inside; another man suffering from ague Butler threw off a balcony into the Thames twenty feet below: 'This surprise absolutely cured him.'

Americans owe the independence of their nation in part to two students of Clare: Charles Townshend who had a 'reputation of brilliance for always doing the opposite of what was expected of him and of what, for that matter, was sensible', and Earl Cornwallis. Townshend as Chancellor of the Exchequer imposed all those taxes which started the American War of Independence and Cornwallis ended it by surrendering to the rebels at Yorktown in 1781.

Two other 18th century students who were also politicians were the Duke of Newcastle and Lord Hervey. Newcastle became Prime Minister as well as Chancellor of the University until 1768 and, though privately uncorrupt, had to learn the evil ways of bribery which was the only way to achieve things in those days. Hervey became Lord Privy Seal and gave Newcastle a very hard time - not the done thing between alumni of the same college - but Hervey got his just deserts when he became known, thanks to the poet Pope, as 'that king of silk, Sporus (effeminate favourite of Nero), that mere curd of Ass's milk.' Not that effeminate since Voltaire wrote his only extant English poem to Hervey's beautiful wife Mary.

Clare produced yet two more eccentrics early in the 20th century. Firstly W.H Fulford, called 'Fluffy' by his friends, who once remarked to Sir Harry Goodwin that 'honeymoons are very nice in their way, but after a few days a man longs for a little intelligent conversation'. Then there was Mansfield Forbes, famous for giving unusual dinner parties: he once searched the surrounding areas to find seven red-haired curates to invite and on another occasion he invited many people with names ending in 'botham' or 'bottom' and left them to introduce themselves ...

The College also boasts the oldest surviving bridge across the river, supposedly built to allow Fellows to leave the College without going into the plague ridden town. It was designed in 1638 by Thomas Grumbold for three shillings, a sum with which he was not in the least happy (he grumbled). His revenge was to leave a segment missing from one of the 14 stone balls on the bridge so that 'the bridge would never be finished'.

ONE OF YOUR BALL
IS DEFICIENT!

Not so long ago, two students made an exact replica in polystyrene of one of the stone balls and, with seemingly great effort, heaved it over the side as a punt full of tourists glided by ... as the tourists shouted in panic, the polystyrene ball gently hit the water and bounced away.

*   *   *

Tourist to guide: 'Now that we've seen the colleges, will you be good enough to show us the University of Cambridge.'

CHRIST'S COLLEGE

William Byngham, a London parish priest, obviously of some means, first founded 'God's House' in 1437 to educate young gentlemen for the lesser degree of Master of Grammar; he hoped to create a new generation of teachers to replace the large numbers killed by the Black Death - it was the front runner of teacher training colleges. However, his means did not stretch far enough and the first Master, John Syclying, persuaded his friend John Fisher who in turn persuaded Lady Margaret Beaufort to finish the College and richly endow it. Fisher was her chaplain and confessor, she was Henry VII's mother, rich and powerful. It was said that she had thirty kings and queens within the four degrees of marriage to her, besides dukes, marquesses, earls and other princes.

She succeeded in founding two colleges, Christ's in 1505 and Saint John's in 1511 but she lived at Christ's for a while and showed her gentle and motherly virtues in urging the Dean to show mercy to her students when dishing out punishment. Lady Margaret must have been sufficiently motherly in other ways as it was also said that by the start of the First World War all of Europe's monarchs were descended from her except King Zog of Albania (surely a minor oversight on her part).

However, it seems she was tough on hygiene as her statutes state that 'if any student or fellow do wipe his hande or fingers of the table clothe, he shall pay for every time one penny'.

11

Almost fifty years later, her great-grandson Edward VI was asked to take away a Fellowship since it was felt that having one Master and twelve Fellows was an imitation of Christ and his twelve Apostles. Edward, cunning for somebody who was so young (he died at 16), stated that he had an easier way to reduce this conceit and added a thirteenth Fellow!

In 1608, James I gave Christ's several hundred mulberry trees, whose leaves are eaten by silk worms, to encourage the silk industry. Only one survived, the famous one under which John Milton used to sleep, dream and compose when he was a student here from 1625. The story goes that one day when Milton was sound asleep under his mulberry tree, a visiting Italian lady saw him and was so struck with his beauty that she wrote some Italian lines to him on a scrap of paper and put it next to his hand. When Milton woke up and found the lines, on being told how they got there, he 'conceived such a passion for the fair unknown' that he eventually went to Italy looking for her and 'thought of her, to the end of his days, as his Lost Paradise'. She was Italian - too disorganised to leave her address. Milton was not happy at University; he described Cambridge as a 'den of formal droanes' and his studies as an 'asinine feast of sow thistles and brambles'. He was not too popular and, being pale and delicate, was called 'the Lady of Christ's'. Lady Margaret would not have approved.

There is a splendid double memorial in the chapel dating from 1684 to two inseparable Fellows, Sir John Finch and Sir Thomas Baines. They were great friends and when Baines died on a visit to Constantinople, Finch had his body embalmed and brought home for burial so that, eventually, they would be together in death also.

Christ's declined in academic standards and general reputation during the next 100 years to the point where a tutor called Gunson said that the place was 'full of slumbering dons' and was desperate for change: 'Fellows knew little and taught even less, dosing over port while waiting for College livings to fall vacant.'..

During the 19th century, standards improved but there was still room for undergraduates to enjoy themselves as was proved by the poet, Charles Calverley, a constant prankster. He had been expelled from Oxford among other things for throwing stones at his college Master's window and continued with his life style in Cambridge. He once stole a pub sign and ran off back to College with the landlord of the pub and an unfriendly crowd in hot pursuit. Calverley hid the sign under his bed and then joined the noisy crowd which had gathered in the court below. On being asked by the Dean what was going on, Calverley replied: 'An evil and adulterous generation seeketh after a sign; and there shall be no sign given it.' (Matthew 12:38)

Our poet hated pomposity and on one occasion he was walking across a lawn when the Provost rebuked him. Calverley seemed to ignore the official who then became rather annoyed and asked: 'Do you know who I am?' Calverley replied that he did not. 'Look again, sir, and tell me what you see before you', whereupon Calverley replied: 'I see an elderly gentleman, apparently very irascible.' His contempt for snobbery was again demonstrated when he came upon a stranger of pompous appearance in the street, stopped him and asked him if he was 'anybody in particular' and whether he, the speaker, had his, the stranger's, permission to remain in the town for the night!

Calverley had to be dragged out of bed by his friends to attend to his studies and always did the bare minimum. He suffered from some brain damage after a fall whilst ice skating and eventually died early of

'Bright's Disease'. Calverley was the boy who never grew up and never fulfilled his earlier promise, but he was a good friend and made people laugh: 'To him seriousness itself was absurdity and he passed through his too brief span of life like an elf, jesting at the grave ways of ordinary mortal men.' A good Cambridge man ...

The 19th century's most famous student must be Charles Darwin who was here from 1825. Darwin had already begun his experiments with nature and although he had not yet specialised, he was already 'zealously collecting beetles'. He once popped a beetle in his mouth so as not to lose track of it whilst his hands were busy with a second beetle, whereupon the first beetle released acid on his tongue and had to be spat out.

At this time, fun rather than learning seemed to be the order of the day. A student called Gunning wrote on entering Christ's in 1784: 'The number of admissions in my year was only three; two of the men professed not to read, and I was ignorant of the first Proposition of Euclid' (it does not seem that bad!). When Gunning became a bedell (university official) he was told that the duties of the office were twofold: to execute the statutes by violating them and to carve well at table. Gunning also said that the College was 'more remarkable for its cordial hospitality than for the refinement of its manners'. A fact borne out by Sir Walter Besant who 'studied moderately and enjoyed himself immensely' and described to a friend a typical day:

'After Hall, men divided into little sets and went in turn to each other's rooms and drank port and sherry till six. I dare say it was not good ... but it generally amounted to only one bottle between four or five men and if it was wrong it was pleasant ...' This came after a 'good honest breakfast with cold pie and beer' and was followed by 'at midnight, when the whist was knocked off, we always sat down to a great supper with copious beer, and after supper to milk punch, and talked till four. And yet some of us survive...'

Some fared less well as was the case with William Perkins who finally gave up drinking on hearing a woman tell her naughty child: 'Hold your tongue, or I will give you to the drunken Perkins yonder.'

CORPUS CHRISTI COLLEGE

Known until 1827 as Bene't College because of the adjacent church, Corpus Christi is unique in that it was founded in 1352 by the townspeople, the members of the guilds of Corpus Christi and of the Blessed Virgin Mary. Students were to 'be trained in academical learning and to pray for the souls of the fraternity members for ever'. It seems that the plague had killed off so many priests that personal entreaties and masses had become very expensive and this seemed a cheap solution to these businessmen!

It was the first college to have a quadrangle, probably to keep in such an expensive investment. The fact that the College was founded by townsmen did not save it from near destruction during the Peasants' Revolt of 1381 when townspeople completely ransacked it and made off with everything that moved including doors and windows ... Complete destruction was avoided through the timely arrival of 'that warlike Bishop of Norwich' who happened to be on his travels armed to the teeth and accompanied by a small army (seemingly a normal routine for bishops in those days); he killed several rioters and unsurprisingly, the rest went home.

ITS CURTAINS FOR ME

However, some of the rioters had already managed to burn the University Charters, led by a mad old woman called Margaret Sterr who threw the ashes up in the air, screaming: 'Thus, thus let the learning of all scholars be confounded.' As a result of the disappearance of all proofs of its origins, Cambridge is now able to claim that it is much older than Oxford since it was founded by Cantaber, a Spanish Prince, years before Christ's birth!

The guilds had perhaps not endowed the College sufficiently as they chose, as its first Master, Thomas de Eltistle 'not that the place might maintain him, but that he the place; being richly beneficed and well seen in secular affairs'.

Soon after came Matthew Parker, Master from 1544 to 1553 who had saved priceless books and manuscripts from destruction during the Dissolution of the Monasteries by Henry VIII. He may not have come by all the books honestly ... but he left his extraordinary collection to his College with the following conditions: it should be kept locked at all times with three keys and only senior Fellows were to be admitted to the library; it would be inspected annually by the Masters and two Fellows of both Gonville and Caius College and Trinity Hall. If any books were missing, the whole collection would go first to Caius and if they failed the inspection it would go to Trinity and then back to Corpus and so on. Corpus still has the collection and the annual inspection has now stopped. The books include King Alfred's copy of 'the Anglo Saxon Chronicle', a Psalter which belonged to Thomas a Becket, a 6th century Gospel believed to have been given by Pope Gregory to Saint Augustine and still used at the enthronement of the Archbishop of Canterbury and 'The Pontifical of the three Bishops' a book in which one of them is 'very arbitrary with three nuns', whatever that means, lucky chap. Despite his generosity, Parker was not popular and although he became Elizabeth I's Archbishop of Canterbury, his body was dug up after his death and thrown onto a dunghill.

Corpus also owns the finest collection of Pre-Reformation (16th century) silver in Cambridge. When other colleges sent their silver plate in the 17th century to support either the King or Parliament during the Civil War, Corpus granted leave of absence to its Fellows as long as they took with them the College plate and hid it until the troubles were over; the College silver was then returned safely. Honest Fellows. The most famous piece of silver is a drinking horn which, still used at College feasts, predates the College and is made from a horn which supposedly used to adorn a long extinct animal - it probably came over with Cantaber ...

In the late 16th century, famous students include Thomas Cavendish, the second man to sail around the world and the two dramatists, Christopher Marlowe and John Fletcher.

Marlowe is reputed to have been a spy for Queen Elizabeth against the French, to have written some of Shakespeare's plays and to have been an atheist (not recommended at the time). A lively, irreverent, gentle man, he was a great figure in Elizabethan drama who died at only 29 in 1593 'assassinated in a Deptford ale house over a bill by a bawdy serving man called Ingram Frizer'. A portrait dated 1585 found earlier this century is presumed to be of him because it says on the picture 'This was him in the 21st year of his age' and Marlowe was 21 in that year. Some may scoff but it seems a reasonable assumption.

John Fletcher also died reasonably young at 46 and is best known for his collaboration with Francis Beaumont on numerous plays. The 'collaboration' was, it seems, total and they were criticised at the time 'for the closeness of their intimacy in that they shared their wardrobe'. It has been said, however, that Elizabethan men were similar to more modern ladies as both were 'avid of new fashions' and if you could not afford it all, why not share, so why should anybody be shocked at poor old Fletcher?

During the same century, Dr Jegon became Master in 1590 and once fined all the students for a collective offence and used the proceeds to whitewash the Hall. This led a student to write:-

Dr Jegon, Bene't College Master
Broke the Scholars' heads and gave the walls a plaister.

And Dr Jegon to reply instantly:-

Knew I the Wag who wrote this verse in Bravery
I'd commend him for his Wit, but whip him for his Knavery.

Despite the popularity of plays promoted by people like Shakespeare, Marlowe and others, it was forbidden at this time to attend or act in plays in Cambridge as is illustrated by the fate of poor old, improbably named, Dominus Pepper. Dominus, as he surely would have liked to have been called by his friends, acted in such a forbidden play at the Black Bear pub in 1600. He was charged with 'being seen with an improper habit, having deformed long locks of unseemly sight and great breeches, indecent for a graduate or scholar of orderly carriage'. The said Dominus was 'commanded to appear in front of the Master, to procure his hair to be cut or powled, which being done, he was then suspended from the College'.

Dominus should have lived in the 1970's when deformed long locks were quite acceptable!

Stephen Hales who was a Fellow from 1703 proved that science was well advanced in the 18th century. He carried out chemistry experiments in a laboratory provided by Trinity and laid 'the foundations of experimental plant and animal physiology'. He was the first to determine with accuracy blood pressure and investigated the movement of sap in plants. Also practical, he improved ways of circulating air artificially in buildings and of preserving food and water on long voyages. Thank god he also had a sense of humour; he published a book entitled 'Friendly admonition to the drinkers of Brandy' in which he promoted temperance by explaining that too much alcohol causes a loss of appetite and enriches the Purveyor of Brandy as opposed to the Grocer!

A less studious man was Thomas Adkin who arrived in 1777. He held dinners which 'were frequent and generally riotous' and he 'neglected everything a man is sent to university to learn'. Adkin was fined £100 for assaulting a man called James Wood who later became the Master of St John's.

There are supposedly two ghosts who haunt the College. The first one is that of Henry Butts, the Master in 1631 when the plague hit again. Everyone fled the College except Butts who stayed to help the sick, which experience drove him mad. Butts hanged himself with his garters two years later - modern day braces would not have been strong enough.

The second ghost is that of young Betts, a student who was wooing, as they say, Dr Spencer's daughter. One story goes that the two young lovers were one day caught in the forbidden library, which housed all Matthew Parker's rare books, by Dr Spencer, Master of the College; Betts was sent down and Spencer's daughter is said to have died soon after from the fright of being caught. The second story again goes that they were wooing in the library, heard Dr Spencer approach and quickly locked Betts in a cupboard whilst the young girl rejoined her father - whereupon the whole College departed on its summer vacation and poor Betts died of starvation in his dusty cupboard.

If the ghost of Betts has been seen, then the second version is true ...
Maybe Betts, surely Butts.

We end as we started with troubles between Town and Gown. J.W
Clark, a student of Corpus in the 1850's wrote about an outing: 'It was
dull work to meet merely for the sake of a boxing match, but a street
disturbance offered an enjoyable diversion, much blood was shed ... and
many heads were broken.'

DOWNING COLLEGE

With such a difficult and inauspicious beginning, things could only improve for Downing College.

It all started with the first Sir George Downing, one time Puritan preacher in 'the Barbadoes' who became Cromwell's Resident at the Hague. A traitor to his King, he then changed his mind as the tide turned and made himself rich and earned himself a title by switching sides and denouncing to King Charles II all his previous Parliamentarian colleagues who were promptly executed. He was called 'a perfidious rogue' by Pepys and 'a frantic preacher not worth a groat' by John Evelyn, another diarist. The one thing for which he is remembered is the building of Downing Street.

His grandson, Sir George Downing, 3rd Baronet was supposedly not much better. He was married at the age of 15 to his cousin Mary aged 13; they never lived together and when she refused to become Queen Anne's lady in waiting, he became cruel to her and eventually divorced her. He was also cruel to his tenants, one of whom hit him on the head with a hammer! At his trial, the poor tenant 'owned the fact, and alleged he thought he did no harm by killing a person who paid nobody, and was so ill a landlord and paymaster with so great an estate'.

Downing died in 1749 having led 'a most miserable, covetous and sordid existence' and without heirs; he left all his money to his cousin Jacob and three other cousins, who all died childless before Jacob, and if there were no heirs, his estate was to be sold to found a college in Cambridge. And then the saga began... Jacob died in 1764 without an heir. His widow Margaret refused to give up the estate and fought legal battles lasting 31 years; she lost the last court case but was allowed to keep the estate during her lifetime. When she died, her second husband fought to keep the money and it was only in 1800 that the Court of Chancery finally decided in favour of Downing's will.

By then a lot of money had obviously gone and the College started poverty stricken when the first stone was laid in 1807.

The worst was over and a new, modern college was born. Downing was the first college to have an American style campus, even before the first in America at the University of Virginia. The statutes were daring, allowing up to half the Fellows to be married, limiting the length of Fellowships and encouraging intercollegiate teaching (presumably because of early staff shortages!) and from the beginning Downing specialised in law and medicine.

In complete contrast to the Founder and his relatives, the first three Masters were learned, gentle and popular. The first, Francis Annesley, was said 'never to have resented an injury and never to have forgotten kindness'. The second, Serjeant Frere, was also successful and popular, bar one argument with the Fellows about keeping his sheep in the courts, with an even more popular wife. Frere's wife had initially shocked the other Masters by giving recitals in her house but she became so liked that on one occasion when she arrived late for a concert it is said that 'all the men and two thirds of the women stood up to offer her a seat'. Frere had trouble staying awake in his old age and would often fall asleep at the dinner table; a comment at the time on a banquet ended with: 'Of course, the Master of Downing slept.'

When Frere died, the obvious successor was Richard Dawes but he was not chosen although he had 'a face so intelligent and benign that children might grow good by looking at it'. The third Master was Thomas Worsley, also a gentle man who would only resort to 'kind expostulations and remonstrances' in his disagreements.

Other people of note included Edward Christian, first Professor of Law and the brother of Fletcher Christian, the leader of the mutineers of the Bounty, and Charles Skinner Matthews and John Perkins.

Matthews was a friend of Byron who once hid in a stone coffin to frighten other guests at one of Byron's house parties. On another occasion Matthews was on a walking trip with his friend Hodgson who became Provost of Eton and, having quarrelled with him, continued the journey in complete silence for approximately 10 miles! Matthews drowned, caught in weeds whilst bathing in the river Cam.

John Perkins was bursar as well as tutor at Downing in the late 1800's and was a good teacher who was extremely popular both on the hunting field and at the dinner table. It was said of him that 'his best memorial to be the great increase in the number of Downing undergraduates whilst he was a tutor and the fact that whilst he was bursar no fox was shot in the College estates', meaning good hunting was had by all. Perkins shot himself in 1901, unable to face progressive blindness.

The College's great eccentric has to be Sir Buswick Harwood who became the first Professor of Anatomy. He was an expert on the sense of smell of fish and told 'obscene' stories. He was supposedly in the habit of burying in his back garden the human leftovers used in his experiments. Harwood became Vice-Master of the College and continued with the Downing down to earth approach. At one breakfast party he seated an undergraduate at the same table as Mansell, the pompous bishop and Master of Trinity. Mansell, thinking himself slighted, rose hurriedly and left.

The next day, Harwood paid a visit to Mansell to inquire whether he had been taken ill.

'I have come, my Lord, on the part of Lady Harwood, as well as on my own, to inquire...' whereupon the Master of Trinity interrupted him: 'Sir Buswick,' he protested, 'I am a prelate of the church, Heaven knows how unworthy...' and this time it was Harwood who interrupted:

'Yes, Heaven does know, my Lord, and so do I' Harwood rejoined, cutting short the preaching, when he realised the reason for Mansell's precipitated exit of the previous day.

*　　*　　*

Preaching was always a popular pastime amongst the clerics of the University. There is the story of the man, once a curate, who bumped into an old friend. Proudly attired in a loud check suit, he announced that he was gloriously happy writing comic songs and that he was about to become a music hall manager in West Australia, 'a position of emolument and responsibility'. About his clerical experiences, the ex-curate admitted that there had been many irksome restrictions: 'But the preaching,' he concluded 'ah, that was scrumptious! All those people sitting stiff as mice while I was gassing!'

EMMANUEL COLLEGE

Emmanuel College was founded in 1584 by one of the great survivors: Sir Walter Mildmay managed to preserve the favours of Henry VIII, his son Edward VI and his dangerous daughters Mary and Elizabeth I, finally becoming Chancellor of the Exchequer for Elizabeth.

The College was to be a 'seed-plot of learned men' and was to breed 'Preachers of the Word' for the new Protestant Church. Building on the site of a former Dominican friary, Mildmay made sure his message got through by turning the friary church into the dining Hall and the monks' refectory into the College Chapel; the present pond was the monks' fishpond and the students' Hostel is naturally built on the foundations of the monastic brewhouse.

Mildmay had great Puritan sympathies and Elizabeth became suspicious; she accused him of having erected a Puritan foundation. Our survivor replied: 'No madam, far be it from me to countenance anything contrary to your established laws; but I have set an acorn which, when it becomes an oak, God alone knows what will be the fruit thereof.'

The students also knew, thanks to Mildmay's statutes which were far from mild and encouraged 'spying': one or two Fellows, at least twice a week, were to visit the students' chambers at night and 'carefully examine what they were doing' - legalised voyeurism - and students were to be stopped from playing, feasting or talking as 'the idle gossip of youths is a waste of time and a bad habit for young minds'. Offenders were to be whipped by the Dean Catechist. In fact, Mildmay only seems to have relaxed at the Feast of Dedication of the College in 1588 when he allowed 'venison from two does and a cragg of sturgeon' to be served for dinner.

WELL IF YOU WEREN'T DOING ANYTHING, YOU'LL HAVE NOTHING TO HIDE,

The first Master of the College was Dr Lawrence Chadderton, one of the translators of King James' Bible. Whilst a student Chadderton had become a Calvinist and his disgusted father had written to him: 'I enclose a shilling in this letter to buy a wallet. Go and beg for a living.' Chadderton did rather well despite his pater's misgivings and became a popular preacher; once, after a two hour sermon, he was about to stop when the congregation shouted 'For God's sake, sir, go on!' How times have changed.... Also a man of action, he saved the life of a student called Richard Bancroft during a violent Town and Gown riot. Bancroft later became Archbishop of Canterbury and whilst he persecuted Puritans and Calvinists everywhere else, he showed his gratitude to his old College by leaving it well alone. Chadderton meanwhile must have been preaching the correct sermon as he died in 1640 aged 103.

Preaching and strong views were popular at Emmanuel. Firstly there was Dr Dell, a master of contradictions. He used to give lengthy sermons against baptism, when all his children were themselves baptised, against universities, when he was himself the Master of a college and against clerics receiving tithes, when he himself took a living of £200 a year. Then there was William Law whose strong Puritan views held that the theatre was 'the place of the Devil's abode'; he himself lived with two old ladies and gave so much money away (probably the old ladies' money) that he attracted to the house all the tramps from miles around.

Samuel Parr, another Fellow, was even worse but had some wit. He insisted on smoking his pipe everywhere, at all times and in all company: 'No pipe, no Parr' he would say and he thought himself so great and important that he allowed himself the rudest of comments and repartees.

On meeting a Welshman called Griffiths, Parr exclaimed: 'A Welshman! I never knew a Welshman who was not a rascal.' To a young Fellow who asked him to collaborate on a book, Parr replied: 'Young man, if all were written in that book which I do know and which you do not know, it would be a very large book indeed.' Our charmer excelled himself in answer to a lady's plea that it was the privilege of women to talk nonsense: 'No madam, it is not their privilege, but their infirmity. Ducks would walk if they could; but nature suffers them only to waddle.'

John Harvard was a student at Emmanuel. He emigrated to New England in America and died there of consumption in 1638. Harvard left half his estate (£779 17s 2d) and 320 books to found a 'schoale at Newetowne' which became Harvard University, the first in America. Out of the first 100 graduates who came to America from England, one third came from Emmanuel, driven out by anti-Puritan feelings.

Puritanism, however, won the day for a while with Cromwell's victory in the mid 1600's and Emmanuel was considered so rightly Puritan that when Masters were imposed on other colleges by Cromwell, eleven of them came from Emmanuel. Another thing which must have made the College unpopular with the rest of Cambridge is that Dowsing,

Cromwell's great destroyer of buildings and artefacts considered not Puritan enough, could find at Emmanuel 'nothing to be amended or done', which meant destroyed - perhaps not such a compliment.

When the Restoration came in 1660, the Master William Sancroft immediately asked Christopher Wren to design a new, more cheerful chapel and made known his intention to remove extreme Puritanism, 'that former singularity which rendered us heretofore so unhappily remarkable'.

Opposite views still prevailed at the College. Dr Richard Farmer, Master from the mid 1700's and a friend of Dr Johnson was extremely learned but indolent and liked nothing better than to turn his rooms into a rallying ground for good talkers. He wrote the book 'Essay on the learning of Shakespeare' which 'inspired savage and opposite views' of the world's favourite bard.

Another man with strange views was Henry Gwatkin, a professor of History from this century: he stated that 'the great age of forgery was from 300 BC to 1700 AD' - whatever forgeries he meant, he gave himself enough leeway but Gwatkin did not take the easy way out when he taught himself German by reading German papers on the 'radulae of snails'.

EIN - RADULAE,
ZWEI - RADULAE,
DREI - RADULAE

Edward Welbourne, Master in 1951, once told a student the joke that 'there are so few Roman Catholics in East Anglia because it is so flat'. Flat land means few railway cuttings and therefore fewer Catholic Irish navvies employed in digging them.... Puritanism dies hard.

*　　*　　*

On the subject of diggings, students one day approached workers who were digging a road and told them that two students dressed as policemen were about to come along and tell them to stop what they were doing. They then accosted two policemen walking nearby and told them that there were students dressed as workers in the next street digging up the road for a laugh....

GONVILLE AND CAIUS COLLEGE

Not unusual in being founded twice, this College has uniquely kept the names of both Founders, yes, Gonville and Caius.

The first, Edmund Gonville, was a Norfolk priest who founded Gonville Hall in 1348 'for the study of theology'. He died three years later leaving little money and therefore little future for his College. The Bishop of Norwich, his executor, moved Gonville Hall nearer his own College of Trinity Hall and renamed it quite simply 'The Hall of the Annunciation of the Blessed Virgin Mary'. The Bishop also changed Gonville's plans in that he wanted students to study law: his view was that it is easier for a clergyman to get along without a knowledge of theology than for a legal functionary to dispense with a knowledge of the law!

AS A THEOLOGIAN, I'M AFRAID I'M A COMPLETE BARRISTER

Gonville carried on in peaceful slumber and genteel decay for almost two hundred years when it was rudely awakened in 1521. Students from the North of England residing in a neighbouring hostel were incited for unknown reasons by their Principal to attack Gonville; they smashed through the gate, rampaged through the buildings, wrecked the buttery including, amazingly enough, all the beer barrels within, and would have completely ruined the College by stealing its silver and plate if the butler had not hidden it all by throwing it into the well. At this point the decay was such that cattle were to be seen wandering through the courts and chapel vestments were being used as bedclothes.

The second Founder was John Kees who Latinised his name to 'Caius' - very chic in those days - and who had been a Gonville student in 1529. Caius studied medicine at Padua University and became physician to Edward VI, Mary Tudor and Elizabeth I, none of whom died happily of old age! This did not stop Caius from becoming President of the Royal College of Physicians nine times; he introduced the study of practical anatomy into England.

Caius, unhappy at the dilapidated state of his old College, obtained a royal charter to refound the College as 'Gonville and Caius College' and became its first Master in 1558. The great man refused to accept payment but imposed strange rules and conditions. The new court should be built on three sides only 'lest the air from being confined within a narrow space should become foul', and there would be three gates to symbolise the academic path: the Gate of Humility, now located meaningfully in the Master's garden, the Gate of Virtue in the centre of the College and used regularly and the Gate of Honour through which students pass on their way to the Senate House to collect their degrees. Caius forbade students to climb roofs and to go to the inn more than twice a year, which instructions, we are told, the students still follow today. He also excluded from admission persons who were 'deaf, dumb, deformed, lame, chronic invalids or Welshmen'! Thank god he was a doctor with an understanding of his fellow man - he probably preferred his fellow man dead and he used to provide many bodies of felons for medical research, perhaps one of the reasons Cambridge became renowned for medicine. Caius was in fact difficult and became unpopular; he would expel or put 'in the stocks' any Fellow who disagreed with him. His Fellows eventually forced him to retire, prompting Caius to write: 'Breed puppies and you will raise wolves.'

The strong medical background was continued with William Harvey,

here from 1593, who discovered the circulation of the blood and wrote a book on the subject in 1628. The book was not well received at first and it was said of him that 'he fell mightily in his practize, and it was beleeved by the vulgar that he was crack-brained'. Edward Wright, a mathematician and Fellow in 1587, was the more likely 'crack-brained'. He asked for sabbatical leave, and was granted it, to join a piratical expedition going to the Azores.

Someone who was forced to leave was John Clarke, Fellow in 1697, for stealing so many books from the University Library that a cart had to be used to bring them all back. Morals were not generally strong in the 17th century but the College survived the Civil War and the Mastership of William Dell, a fiery puritan who was eventually accused after the Restoration of allowing a tinker to preach in his church. The 'tinker' was in fact John Bunyan (Pilgrim's Progress), the son of a tinker, who had preached a sermon in which he had said that

Cambridge was composed of no more than 'stews of Antichrist and dens of thieves'.

A truly worse son of a bad father was Titus Oates, here in the mid 1600's, the famous perjurer and fabricator of the Popish plot in which Oates caused the execution of some thirty five innocent people falsely accused of plotting to assassinate Charles II. Oates senior had certainly been a bad example; he was a charlatan Baptist preacher, known as 'Dipper', who would charge 10 shillings a time to baptise simpleton housemaids in the nearest stream, at midnight, even in freezing weather, until one died of shock. Titus was himself caught with a stolen gown and was expelled after denying the deed with 'horrid imprecations'. Desperate to obtain a degree, he finally bought one from Salamanca University!

TRUST ME DEARIE, I'M A BAPTIST

One can understand the Bishop of Durham, a former student and contemporary of all of the above, endowing the College in 1660 with scholarships but insisting that they should be for 'studious, short-haired men'. He could not have specified 'humble bachelors' as the last 17th century Master of Caius,

Dr Thomas Gooch would not have approved. It was said of Gooch that he was a man 'of as great art, craft and cunning as any in the age he lived in' which qualified him to become eventually the Bishop of Ely. A tablet in the Chapel commemorates Gooch and testifies to his being an 'unashamed pluralist in wives no less than in ecclesiastical preferments'.

The 18th century saw the arrival of many learned men at Caius, though what they found to read is not obvious as proved by the young German called, with the usual Teutonic brevity, Zacharias Conrad Von Uffenbach, who came to visit in 1710. He asked the librarian to show him the room where valuable and ancient manuscripts were kept and he was taken to 'a miserable garret under the roof, which could have been very little or not at all visited, for the top step was buried in pigeons' dung, and the manuscripts lay thick with dust on the floor and elsewhere in total disorder'.

Nevertheless, there was Dr Vince, Fellow in mathematics, brilliant but eccentric and rather literal minded. He was invited to tea at a house in a London square but failed to show up. On being asked why he did not come, he replied that he had come but having found that the square was in fact a parallelogram, he went away again. The statues of other worthies can be seen on the outside of the College walls, gazing down upon the bicycle accidents in Trinity Street: among them are William Hyde Wolleston who was known as 'the Pope' because of the infallible results of his physics and chemistry experiments and Jeremy Collier who ruined British drama in the 18th century with his book 'Short View of the Immorality and Profaneness of the English Stage.'

Then came the students, here for a good time and only a little learning. When asked by the Dean why he was wearing gaudy coloured cuffs when the law specifically disallowed any cuffs of gay colour being attached to the students' 'subfusc' coat (the black gown), Lord Thurlow proved that his cuffs were attached not to his coat but to his waistcoat ... on another occasion when the same Dean set him Greek work to do, Thurlow went to see a different tutor with his work to see if he had made any mistakes as he reckoned the Dean's Greek to be below par and he wanted to submit his work to an 'expert'; this time Thurlow was asked to leave. Years later he became Lord Chancellor. Frank Lockwood became Solicitor-General after much the same career at Caius. He was sent down after, among other things, being out at midnight 'oddly attired in flannels and the gown of a Master of Arts, performing strenuously upon some blatant instrument of music'. Being a very big man, he overwhelmed the policeman asked to arrest him. Lockwood came back later disguised as an 'interested' foreigner and succeeded in persuading his old tutor to take him on a guided visit of the College culminating in dinner at the high table with the other Fellows 'where he sat winking at his old student friends'.

BLATANT INSTRUMENT MAN!
SHAME ABOUT THE FLANNELS

A student from another college wrote about Caius in the 19th century:

'Know ye the College where men never shine
In aught but in quaffing the juice of the vine?'

Not fair if one takes into account the mathematics tutor, Thomas Manning, who pondered on 'the mysterious empire of China', learned Chinese and visited Canton in 1806. Manning was the first Englishman to 'penetrate Lhasa' and he played chess with the Dalai Lama. What about Dr Wilson, a student here in the late 1900's, who was part of Scott's ill fated expedition and who flew the College flag at the South Pole? That same flag is now kept in the College Hall.

Effort of a different kind was needed in 1921 when over 120 Caius students were involved in stealing an artillery piece given by the War Office to Jesus College as a souvenir. It took six hours to drag the heavy piece out of Jesus College, through railings which had been cut and down several steps into Caius. It was also the night that the Master of Caius was entertaining the Bishop of Ripon to dinner. The Master, having heard a noise, glanced out of the window; startled, he then asked the Bishop to look out himself and tell him whether he saw anything.
'Yes, Master, I see a gun', said the Bishop.
'Thank goodness,' said the Master, 'so do I.'
It seems that 'the physical' was important at Caius at this time. Thomas Oakley a Fellow in the 1920's recalled a discussion with a visiting headmaster about possible recruits to the College. The hierarchy talked about the current students 'only in relation to their prowess at Rugby ... not a word was said about their learning. Double firsts were not talked about.'

Finally, an example of Caius statutes, forbidding climbing, being studiously obeyed. There was allegedly in the 1950's a 'Nocturnal Climbing Society' whose members risked life and limb leaping from the roof of the College onto the roof of the Senate House - for fun and thrills, of course. The story goes that in 1958, engineering students belonging to the society dismantled a small van and reassembled it overnight onto the roof of the Senate House, having brought every piece of the van across the roofs. After being a star attraction for most of the next day, it was removed by government workers after much difficulty and a great deal of equipment.

JESUS COLLEGE

There were only two nuns left in 1496 in the impoverished Benedictine nunnery of Saint Radegund; one was allegedly with child, the other but a child. John Alcock, Bishop of Ely, described as 'given from his childhood to learning and religion; so growing from virtue to virtue that no one in England was more reputed for his holiness' was the worst possible visitor to the nunnery! Alcock said that 'only two nuns remain. One is elsewhere and the other is of ill fame' and he accused them of 'improvidence, extravagance and incontinence'; he totally curtailed their enjoyment by closing down the convent and getting a licence from Henry VII to found 'the College of the Blessed Mary the Virgin, St John the Evangelist, and the glorious Virgin St Radegund' - a

physical state not suffered by her nuns. Perhaps in order not to leave out anybody too important, the College has always been known as Jesus College. Continuing with the logical theme, the long, narrow, high walled path leading to the gate tower is called 'The Chimney' and the College coat of arms, in memory of John Alcock, incorporates three cocks, the male counterparts of hens.

Archbishop Cranmer was the most famous student and Fellow in the 16th century, although things did not go too well for him either at the beginning or at the end. As a student he said 'he was nursled in the grossest kind of sophistry, logic, philosophy and the dark riddles of Duns…' and later, when a Fellow, he fell in love and married 'Black Joan', a barmaid at the local Dolphin Inn; since Fellows were supposed to be celibate and sleep in College, Cranmer resigned his Fellowship until Black Joan died in childbirth within a year and he could become a Fellow again.

Cranmer made a lot of money during his lifetime and was eventually appointed Archbishop of Canterbury by Henry VIII, a position he did not want but Henry insisted and as Cranmer himself said 'it was as fatal to refuse Henry's favours as to offer him injuries', so he accepted! Then came Mary Tudor: Cranmer at first recanted his Protestant faith in favour of Mary's Catholicism but when he changed his mind again, he became one of the great reformers educated at Cambridge and burnt at the stake in Oxford on her orders in 1556. This very 'human' man felt ashamed at the earlier betrayal of his faith and when the final fire was lit, he thrust his right hand first into the flames 'in order that the offending member which had signed the recantation might perish first'.

Peace returned briefly to Jesus in the 17th century and when James I came to visit Cambridge, he chose to 'pray at King's, eat at Trinity and study and sleep at Jesus' which is slightly out of the way and therefore more quiet. During the Civil War, Jesus, like most colleges, supported James' son, Charles I and as a result when the latter lost, two of the Fellows were arrested whilst the others voted themselves a holiday and fled Cambridge having delayed only long enough to bury the chapel organ in the Master's orchard.

From this period dates the autographed copy of the first edition of the first Bible printed in America which is in the Old Library. It was printed in 1663 in Cambridge, Massachussetts, in Algonquin and translated by John Eliot, a Jesus man who went to America to convert North American Indians to Christianity. Other worthies of the period include Tobias Rustat a great benefactor, whose father was at Jesus and who was described by the diarist Evelyn as 'a very simple, ignorant but honest and loyal creature' - better than being ignored as Oscar Wilde would have said - and the elegant Foley who 'affected a scarlet coat because it was denounced in the statutes' and lastly, 'ghastly' Castley who 'enjoyed the humours of a merry-go-round arranged in a great coat of tolerably bright green'. Two lovely sights which cannot have lasted long in the College.

MORE LIKE 'BOUNCY' CASTLEY IF YOU ASK ME

The 18th century was Jesus' literary period. Firstly, there was the Reverend T.R Matthews, Fellow, who wrote anonymously a book called 'Essay on the Principle of Population' which was so negative about a forthcoming population explosion against an insufficient food supply that it was described as a book which 'portends to the timid the very gravest catastrophes'.

Then came Laurence Sterne (author of Tristram Shandy) as a student in 1733. He was not too keen on hard work and approved of his tutor whom he described in a letter as 'having sense as he did not trouble me with trammels (nonsense)' and that this neglect from his tutor, he himself rewarded with gratitude! Sterne liked to sit lazily under a Walnut tree in the Cloister Court and wrote this verse about the tree:

At Cambridge many years ago,
In Jesus was a Walnut tree;
The only thing it had to show,
The only thing folk went to see...

Finally came Samuel Taylor Coleridge in 1791 who wrote of the 'quiet ugliness of Cambridge' and who left with no degree - not surprising when one considers how busy he was at being bad. He was once found drunk in the gutter with another friend and on being offered help he shouted: 'Save my friend, I can swim.' On another occasion Coleridge was the general in charge of a party of inebriated students on a mission to punish an apothecary for performing too speedy a cure on Newton, their maths tutor, who had fallen and half drowned in a duck pond the week before. During proceedings in the Senate House resulting in the expulsion of the Unitarian Fellow of the College, W. Frend, whom he admired, Coleridge proclaimed his support with loud applause. One of the Proctors, wishing to apprehend the perpetrator of this vile action, carefully noted the place from which this noise came in the gallery and proceeded to it. Coleridge, however, had noticed this manoeuvre and immediately gave up his place to another student; the latter was then seized by the Proctor and accused of 'unseemly clamour caused by clapping hands' until, the likely story goes, the innocent student stood up and exclaimed: 'Alas, would that that were possible.' He showed himself to be an armless cripple...

Coleridge drew up plans with his two friends, Lovell and Southey, for a 'socialistic settlement in America' and since they needed wives for the venture he hastily became engaged to Sarah Fricker whose two sisters were in turn engaged to his two friends. The plans came to nothing but Coleridge had to depart hurriedly from Jesus to escape debts and he joined the army under the name of Silas Tomkins Cumberback - and why not? Coleridge, surprisingly enough, was persuaded by his College to leave the army and return to Cambridge which he nevertheless finally left without a degree.

Students have always complained about the food. Coleridge once remarked to a Fellow during a meal: 'We have veal, Sir, tottering on the edge of beef.' Later a petition was signed by students in 1871 asking for 'properly cooked meat from the usual joints of recognised animals!'

Such complaints always fall on deaf ears and the University historian, D.A Winstanley, spoke for all educational establishments when he wrote: 'College authorities are not apt to be deeply stirred by complaints of the Hall dinner, being so accustomed to them.'

Jesus became a great rowing college, a reputation which started under the Mastership of Dr Corrie, elected Master in 1849. Corrie was asked to support the growth of sport in general in Cambridge and actually said: 'I will gladly support you but you must not ask me for support for rowing, an occupation to which I can give no countenance, owing to the bedizened women on the bank.' Despite his attitude, Jesus excelled in this sport to such an extent that one of the Fellows complained that 'the College is becoming nothing but a boat club'.

The reputation for being a 'rowing' not an 'intellectual' college persisted into the 20th century and was actively encouraged by proud alumni. In the late 1940's, some alumni read in the Times newspaper that 'Jesus was no longer Head of the River and that Jesus men were getting firsts in their degrees' and they formed a deputation to visit the Master to register their disapproval...

KING'S COLLEGE

King's College seems to have an excess of everything: an excess of Founders, of learned and useless men, of the good and the bad, of the strange ...

Henry VI founded Eton College in 1440 when he was 18 years old and the year after founded at Cambridge the 'College of Saint Nicholas' for twelve students; he then expanded his vision and decided to build his College on a much grander scale, for 70 students (the number of Christ's earliest missionaries) and renamed it 'The King's College of Our Lady and Saint Nicholas'.

Among other things, the King's statutes did not permit loitering in Hall, fishing and the keeping of 'unwanted or rarely seen wild beasts such as monkeys, bears, stags or foxes'. Students had to be clean shaven and porters would shave off beards and moustaches, which were disallowed until 1859. Students were allowed dogs which most of them kept and a few had horses; Montague Norman, one of the first governors of the Bank of England, came up in 1889 but actually left the College after one year because the stabling accommodation was inadequate.

GOT ANY WILD ANIMALS TUCKED AWAY IN THERE 'AVE WE SIR?

The statutes also required that only Etonians were admitted as students; they had special privileges at Cambridge such as obtaining degrees without taking examinations and not being subject to the Proctors' authority. This caused so much jealousy that King's College was attacked in 1454 by other students 'with guns and habiliments of war', but it was only in 1871, after more than 400 years, that non Etonians were finally admitted. Mind you, not without some resistance: Robbie Ross, a friend of Oscar Wilde and a well known aesthete, was criticising as late as 1889 the prevalence of Old Etonians at King's, was thrown into a fountain for his pains, suffered a serious breakdown as a result and only after that was a full integration of Etonians and non Etonians complete!

Back to Henry VI. Poor, gentle, saintly Henry did not see his plans completed as he was deposed in 1461 and eventually murdered in the Tower of London in 1471; he had inherited two great kingdoms from his father, England and France, and had lost both in his lifetime but he had meanwhile founded two of Britain's greatest colleges in Eton and King's.

It took a further four Kings to complete Henry's magnificent College and Chapel, Edward IV, Richard III, Henry VII and Henry VIII who even paid for some stained glass windows in the Chapel himself! The Chapel has the largest fan vaulted stone ceiling in the world and is reckoned to be the finest Gothic building in Europe. The world famous King's choir is made up of 16 choristers who wear the Eton uniform, collars and top hats, and 14 undergraduates. They have sung in hundreds of services every year except when the Puritans under Cromwell suppressed them. Maybe there was a reason for that as in 1636 Archbishop Laud's commission complained about the choir: 'Some of the quiremen cannot sing and are divers of them very negligent. The choristers are near one half of them mutes.'

Talking about Cromwell, his henchman Dowsing, who was in charge of destroying all buildings and artefacts not considered Puritan enough in the 17th century (once the Civil War had been won by the

Parliamentarians), had a field day in Cambridge. When he came to King's Chapel, it is said that 'the prospects of so much smashing quite discomposed his faculties...' However, according to the College accounts, he was paid off 6s 8d to leave the building alone - it must have been only the top of a hidden bribery iceberg.

A more subtle form of bribery was carried out by the College when Henry VI took over compulsorily a thriving part of the Town to create the present unused but attractive land at the back of King's, called the 'Backs'. This created bad relations with the Town which agreed to the surrender of the land on condition that is was put to good use; so the College, to this day, keeps five grazing bullocks in its back garden.

King's College is now completed and looks according to John Ruskin like 'a table upside down with its four legs in the air' which refers to the four tall structures on each corner connected by high walls, to get over which the less agile student returning late at night needs the night porter to lend a shoulder.

The 16th century was very dangerous for the men of King's, especially the principals of the College, the Provosts. John Argentine, Provost from 1501 to 1508 was also the doctor in charge of the two little Princes in the Tower of London and was the last man to see them alive - except for the murderer of course - a fact which probably put his own life at risk. Another perilous duty for Provosts was to go on a circuit on horseback to visit Eton and the College manors: on one such journey Halton, Provost from 1508 to 1509 nearly had his throat cut by a thief whilst sleeping under a tree and Altrinson, Provost from 1553 to 1556, actually died of the plague on his journey.

One of the advantages of being Provost was the comfortable Provost's lodge which was so agreeable that Elizabeth I would have stayed longer during her visit in 1564 'if the beer had not run out'. She was probably happy with the other conveniences as her godson, John Harrington, was

NOT NOW... I'M OFF FOR A BEER

FLUSH

at the College, the man who is reputed to be the inventor of the water closet.

Elizabeth's host on that visit was Provost Philip Baker a 'crypto Catholic' who was let off in 1565 for possessing Popish books, ornaments and vestments. Four years later he committed the same offences and before his arrest, managed to flee overseas but being an honest man, he returned the College horses on which he had fled and the College silver with which one inevitably travelled!

Puritan sentiment ruled the day and, for example, the wearing of a surplice in chapel was obligatory but not popular. One undergraduate was caught not wearing his surplice and pleaded conscientious objection; he eventually admitted that he had 'run into debt for his belly' and had pawned his surplice to the cook. Another disreputable youth was Nicholas West who committed arson in the Provost's lodge; he eventually became Bishop of Ely and a great benefactor to the College.

John Greenhall, a scholar who left in 1579 in his third year, did not become anything; he was arrested for highway robbery shortly after and was hanged and dissected. The late 16th century saw the arrival of the hated strict disciplinarian Provost Roger Goad. He had banned football as unscholarly and swimming in the river carried the penalty of the 'birch'. In 1603, when the plague was in London, he feared it coming to Cambridge and so dispersed the College whereupon some poor scholars had nowhere to go but back to London to live and teach. When works were being carried out in the chapel crypt in the early 20th century, Goad's coffin accidentally fell open to reveal an empty coffin bar a boar's tusk - one can imagine what his students had done with his body.

The early 17th century was a period of disorder and decline at King's. There had been riots in 1596 and 1606 when students were denied admittance to oversold comedies (the only real entertainment in Town at the time) and there was such a shortage of money that places at the College were bought. Two bursars absconded with the College funds and a third 'went off ... on the account of a bastard being laid to him' and he 'changed his name being in danger of the laws'. A second man willing to change his name was Roger Palmer; he was created Lord Castlemaine for not noticing his wife's affair with Charles II. Then the good came along. Firstly Samuel Collins, Provost from 1615 to 1645, who was a kindly man and great wit. He was imprisoned by the Parliamentarians for supporting Sunday games and giving a larger piece of consecrated bread to hungry communicants! His successor Benjamin Whichcote was broad minded, moderate and liberal and gave half his stipend to poor old banished Collins. Junior members caused him trouble by sneaking against his royalist Fellows but Whichcote finally won when he 'caught one (troublemaker) too familiar with his laundress's daughter and turned him out'.

Another Fellow was Anthony Ascham who wrote an ingenious treatise 'in favour of siding with the emerging power'. Cromwell rewarded him by making him Ambassador in Madrid where he was murdered in 1650 by Royalists. Serves him right. Some people must have believed in Divine Retribution in this, the period of Divine Rights of Kings, as Provost Sir Thomas Page found out in 1681. He was the first layman Provost and died suddenly whilst reprimanding an undergraduate for his infrequent attendance at chapel.

At the end of the century, King William decided to foist his own choice as Provost on the College in direct contradiction to the statutes. United as one, the Fellows refused and, rising to the occasion, they were unbelievingly 'prepared to sell their plate and forego their second course at dinner to pay for court fees'. Faced with such determination, William desisted.

Morals and hard work were not in much evidence at the beginning of the 18th century. Horace Walpole, son of Sir Robert Walpole - the first Prime Minister of Britain and a student at King's in the 1690's - was told in 1735 by his tutor, the blind professor Sanderson: 'Young man, it would be cheating you to take your money for you can never learn what I am trying to teach you.' Horace cried a little, then decided to enjoy himself.

It was about these times that the poet Thomas Gray wrote: 'The men at King's are a sort of University by themselves ... everybody hates them.' There were all sorts of scandals. One Fellow gave up his Fellowship to elope with Walpole's daughter-in-law, then dumped her and died destitute in Italy. Another Fellow, William Moore, got himself so deeply into debt in the 1780's that he had to ride everywhere in order to escape his creditors more efficiently; having fled to Suffolk where he was soon in debt to local tradesmen, Moore came back to Cambridge and earned a living writing travelogues about countries to which he had never been. Then there was the Fellow who pawned his Fellowship against cigars and port, and also the bursar who, having fled the College with the cash, was mistakenly arrested in London for a wanted criminal and immediately dropped dead of shock. Divine Retribution again.

The students were not much better. One undergraduate, presumably not well-behaved, fled the College 'in apprehension his Fellowship would be denied him' and afterwards kept 'that infamous coffee shop in Covent Garden' - probably frequented by many ex-bursars and ex-Fellows of King's! A few years later Harry Matthews, another student and an old Etonian who owed Eton a great deal of money spent on hiring boats and guns, was hunted down to King's by Charlie Carter, the bursar of Eton. The bursar was plied with wine and beer by Matthews until he passed out whereupon Matthews sewed him inside a greatcoat and put him on the mail coach back home... The student never heard of the bursar again.

AND THERE'S A JAM SANDWICH IN THE POCKET

There was also a shortage of money at this time. William Fleetwood, who became Bishop of Ely, wrote the first treatise on inflation in 1707 to justify a departure from the statutes and allow Fellows, of whom he was one, to keep their Fellowship stipends even if they also had a private income in excess of £5. The lack of money made people more devious... Lord Godophin, on hearing that the antechapel needed repaving and that the College could not afford it, surrendered to King's a debt of £400 owed to him by a Mr Pemberton who was refusing to pay up. Since this sum was so important, some undergraduates ran Mr Pemberton to earth at the Rose Inn, kidnapped him and only let him free once the debt had been settled! What devotion to one's College.

However, there was no shortage of famous and infamous people. There was George Stevens, the quarrelsome friend of Dr Johnson, an exposer of literary forgeries, begetter of two of his own and the first scholarly editor of Shakespeare - even if he added obscene footnotes and falsely attributed them to a clergyman. Also William Goldwin, student in 1700 who became a headmaster and produced the first literary work entirely devoted to the game of cricket and how it is played (in Queen Anne's time, of course); it is called 'In Certaimen Pilae' and consists of ninety five hexameters.

What about Sir William Draper, a superb cricketer and the only Fellow to win a battle. He raised his own infantry regiment and fought gallantly during the defence of Madras. He captured Manila in 1762 in a ten day campaign; he proved that education sometimes pays off as he had to negotiate with his opponent, a defeated Spanish Bishop, in Etonian Latin.

A little later came the best known tutor of his time, the Reverend Charles Simeon, Fellow from 1782 to 1836. As a student, he was told he had to be ordained because he was so good at preaching, a fact he proved many years later when he replaced a vicar who was on holiday. Simeon used to fill the church, such were his sermons, so that on his return, the vicar was told by his parish clerk: 'Ah sir, I am so glad you have come back. Now we shall have room again!'

Simeon became bursar, dean and Vice-Provost in turn and was at first a lonely and sometimes forbidding figure. He used to pray on the roof of Gibbs' building so that 'no eye but the Supreme can behold me'. He became a wildly popular and influential preacher because he refused to compromise; a fellow bursar once asked him 'why do you call me an atheist? I never called you a humbug'. Simeon also refused to remain on speaking terms with a clerical colleague called Edward Pote because the latter never attended chapel and once actually conducted a funeral service in his shooting gear with his gun and dogs waiting outside for a day's hunting.

In those days, absenteeism from chapel was punishable by having to write a Latin epigram which, most of the time, was normally good for a year's transgressions!

Definitely a good churchgoer was John Bird Sumner, a student in 1798. He was described by Samuel Wilberforce as 'good, gentle and weak and could never decide how to vote' not a plus for someone who became

Archbishop of Canterbury and the last Bishop to wear a wig in church.

Good news does not sell so let us end the 18th century with a catalogue of rogues who illustrate the lax standards still prevailing at the time. There was Provost Cooke who melted down a 300 year old College cup to make 'an urn of silver for his wife's tea table'. Scrope Davies, friend of Byron, who had to escape his creditors early in his life and went off to live in Calais where he died in 1852 with his Fellowship still his only source of income. Finally Caleb Colton, Fellow from 1797 until 1818; he was among other things, a parson, wine merchant, gambler and wearer of military uniforms (nurses did not exist then). He also had to live abroad, naturally, but returned once a year to King's for a one night stay and attendance at one chapel service, which entitled him to retain his Fellowship, before fleeing back to much visited Calais from where he criticised the immorality of Byron's Don Juan in a pamphlet!

The 19th century saw changes in old patrician habits: Fellows had to live in Cambridge and the Dean of King's could no longer ride to hounds direct from chapel. Some bad habits die hard, though, and there was a last flurry of problems with morals. In 1850 the choristers were shocked by the irreverent talk among Fellows during the Creed and a Fellow was suspended for two years for seducing a respectable woman who was asking only for a chapel ticket. Henry VI and Archbishop Laud would not have been pleased. Finally, when it was announced in 1882 that Fellows were now allowed to marry if they had held their Fellowship for over 10 years, some of them alleged that they had met their wives from the next London train!

The good men included the Reverend Henry Battiscombe, here in 1820, the reputed inventor of the roller skate, and Provost Richard Oakes. He was a genial and courteous gentleman with strong views. When the Lord Chief Justice came on a visit, Oakes was 'not at home' to him. He explained that his Lordship was 'a very Clever man but not at all a Good man' and so he did not want to see him. Clever but naïve about students, Oakes asked in pained surprise a scholar who had totally misread a New Testament lesson in chapel 'why he had not consulted the original in Greek beforehand'.

Oscar Browning had been expelled from Eton where he was a housemaster for being too arrogant and generally too familiar with the boys. He became a Fellow at King's (not such a demanding role ...) became both popular and rather fat as this ode illustrates:

> *O.B, oh be obedient*
> *To Nature's stern decrees;*
> *For though you be but one O.B,*
> *You may be too obese.*

He was such a big eater and drinker that he would set his alarm clock for 3am so that he could drink a quick bottle of ale before falling asleep again.

Browning's arrogance led him to profess he knew everybody and he once said that the 'German Emperor was about the pleasantest emperor he had met'. A few interesting students at the College in the 19th century include Stratford Canning who came up in 1805, Eustace Miles in 1887 and L.F Giblin in 1893.

Stratford Canning, cousin of George Canning the Prime Minister, was the British attaché in Constantinople at the age of 24. He engineered a treaty between the Turks and Russia so that Russia could be free to fight Napoleon. Later in 1842, he persuaded the Turks to abolish the use of torture and to fight Russia, which was the major cause of the Crimean War. 'A look at his portrait in the Dining Hall, painted when he was over 90, helps to explain the Turks' subservience', wrote a later wit.

Eustace Miles was a classics coach, world tennis champion, writer on hygiene and reincarnation and founder of a chain of vegetarian restaurants. L.F Giblin came from Tasmania, played rugby for England, he became Professor of Economics, Member of the Tasmanian Parliament, a great soldier who made his own bow ties and knew the two approved ways of saddling a pack mule ...

The 20th century started peacefully with people like Hamilton Hartridge, here in 1905, whose Gibbs' rooms were full of bats. Hartridge stretched silk threads across the outer room and noted the bats' evasive tactics when faced with a blocked exit; this led him to understand the characteristics of echo sounding which foreshadowed 'sonar', Britain's great ally in later wars. The pathetic results of war can be seen in the Chapel where there is a memorial to all those who fell in the First World War, including King's famous son, the poet Rupert Brooke; slightly apart there is an inscription to 'Pensioner, Ferenc Bekassy', a Hungarian student at King's who died fighting for the Germans.

In 1914, J.T Sheppard became a Classics tutor, despite being given a bad reference earlier in his youth: 'Mr Sheppard has an unfortunate lightness of touch. This might be cured by a year in a German seminar.' Not the most timely of opinions or suggestions. Sheppard became Vice-Provost, gave great lectures and was good fun, so much so that John Raymond Keynes wrote in a letter that Charlie Chaplin had not been as much fun at a party as the Vice-Provost. Keynes, who became Lord Keynes the respected economist, had come up in 1902 and had written in yet another letter: 'I've had a good look round the place and come to the conclusion that it's pretty inefficient.'

Inefficient but still fun ... Over the years countless attempts have been made to climb the Chapel's pinnacles and roofs - a 1760 coin was found on a ledge below the summit of one pinnacle. Students placed an umbrella on another in 1932; the porters helped a student onto the Chapel roof so that he could blast it down with his shotgun. When two Union Jacks appeared in the umbrella's place the next day, the student refused to shoot them down on account of his patriotism ... and steeplejacks had to be sent for, at substantial cost.

The students' 'cheek' went further in 1965 when several climbers managed to hang between the spires a banner reading 'Peace in Vietnam'. The next day, the dean received a letter informing him that the roof was in an extremely dangerous state and unless work was carried out forthwith, the safety of future climbers could not be guaranteed!

MAGDALENE COLLEGE

It was first called 'Monks' Hostel' and was built in 1428 by the Abbot of Crowland, soon to be joined in his venture by the Abbeys of Ely, Ramsey and Walden. The purpose was to house and properly supervise their young men studying at Cambridge with such realistic rules as 'the students of this College are to visit taverns less often than other students'.

Then came Henry, 2nd Duke of Buckingham who endowed the College, but not enough, before he was executed for treason in 1483, and Monks' Hostel became Buckingham College. His son Edward, 3rd Duke of Buckingham next endowed the College but again not sufficiently before he too was executed for treason in 1521. Twenty years later came Thomas, Baron Audley of Walden who again endowed the College but again not sufficiently before his early death two years later at the age of 56; he renamed Buckingham College 'The College of St Mary Magdalene' in 1542 which, pronounced 'Maudlin', is a play on his name 'Audley'. Finally, Audley's son in law the Duke of Norfolk took his fate in his hands and promised the College £40 a year only to be beheaded for treason in 1572. Not surprisingly, after what someone called 'the wholesale liquidation of its benefactors', Magdalene

£40 A YEAR? STEADY!... DON'T GO LOSING YOUR HEAD

suffered for centuries from a lack of funds and endowments.

Audley, the most important of the benefactors, retained for his descendants the right to select the Master. He was a difficult and unpopular man, Henry VIII's Lord Chancellor who had presided over the trials of Sir Thomas More and Anne Boleyn and had got rid of two other wives and Thomas Cromwell for the King. Audley is buried in an altar tomb of black marble of which it was written:
'The stone is not harder nor the marble blacker than the heart of him who lies beneath.'
Although one student was pleased with his room, writing the graffito 'formosum antrum' on his wall, the 16th century continued to be a disaster for the College as a whole. A certain Benedict Spinola, financial adviser to Magdalene, persuaded the College to sell 'worthless land' through a middleman to himself and promptly disappeared a rich man... there is now a gargoyle of him with water able to gush out of its mouth into the river, symbolising the drivel of advice Spinola gave. Later on, the College 'pawned' seven acres in the City of London in a deal which was probably illegal; the acres became so valuable that Barnaby Goche of Magdalene and the Senior Fellow tried to retrieve the land through court actions, lost and ended up in gaol. Matters became so bad that a Master of the time, Degory Nichols, had to keep cows which grazed outside the Hall and sometimes strayed inside during meals.

But all was not lost as the gateway leading to Benson Court illustrates; it dates from this period and has carvings which suggest that it was a house of ill repute as 'one can discern a seated man, a naked woman and a Centaur, all in a state of sexual excitement', so describes a 19th century visitor.

There were no new benefactors until the mid 1600's and bad times continued until the mid 1700's with only a small number of students, actually less than ten, a visiting German noted only about 600 books, all covered in mould, but the College somehow acquired a bit of a reputation for virtues which ranged 'from godliness to good hunting'. It must have included the usual drinking as a Master was reprimanded by the visiting Archbishop of Canterbury for drunkenness and was punished with four days' abstinence; as a result the Master promptly dropped dead.

All this must have driven Henry Dunster to emigrate to America: he was one of the two founders of Harvard University and its first President. Dunster was President of Magdalene College, which means second in command to the Master, and must have carried the title with him to America, expecting a 'Master' to be appointed over him at Harvard. This never happened and to this day, thanks to Magdalene, the title 'President' remains attached to most top positions in America.

The great diarist Samuel Pepys came up to Magdalene in 1651 having won two scholarships. He was a heavy drinker and was once 'scandalously observed with drink' which earned him a serious reprimand. This was not enough to upset him and when he died in 1703 he left his extensive library to the College on condition that the 3000 volumes should be kept as inherited: no new purchases, no sales. They were to be kept in his own specially designed bookcases, probably the first with glass panels and were catalogued by size with the smaller volumes standing on wooden blocks to make all the books level. The collection includes six volumes of Pepys' famous diaries, all in shorthand which the Reverend John Smith of St John's spent three years deciphering at the end of which, bless his heart, he found a key to the shorthand in the library!

Another studious 18th century student was Richard Cumberland who became Bishop of Chester and learned the Coptic language when 80 years old. Peter Peckard, Master in 1785, was one of the earliest advocates for the suppression of the slave trade; in chapel, instead of the usual bidding prayers, he would shock his listeners by asking for prayers 'for their brethren in the West Indies labouring under galling conditions'.

MUST BE WRITERS' BLOCKS

Peckard's example surely influenced all the students who became missionaries during the next century to Africa, Australia, and India and Sir Charles Vyner Brooke, student in 1894, 3rd white Raja of Sarawak who was 'keen to punish head hunters'. Good show.

Another good influence was the preacher Simeon who reversed the College's reputation in 1866 'for a luxurious table and very lax discipline'; religion was back in and drink was out and Magdalene's students became well known 'for their temperate habits and devotion to tea', so much so that some wag wrote that 'the Cam which bathed the very walls of the College is said to have been rendered unnavigable by tea leaves'.

The College is said to have stagnated under its Master, the Reverend the Honourable Latimer Neville, brother of the College's patron Lord Braybrooke; Latimer is supposed to have slumbered in his lodge from

1853 to 1904! A state of mind well understood by the distracted professor Reverend William Farish who on one occasion mounted the horse brought by his servant, dismounted it again on the other side and was walking away in deep thought when the shouts of his servant brought him back to start his journey again. He held the Chair of Chemistry and was Professor of Natural and Experimental Philosophy which was qualification enough for him to assure the promoters of the Manchester and Liverpool Railway that 30 miles per hour was a safe speed and 60 mph could be done!

The College was still poor in the 19th century and could only afford to build part of a grandiose Lutyens scheme. Economies were forced upon the famous architect in 'The Lutyens Building' and his retaliatory joke was to design different banisters in all the staircases 'to help the Magdalene men feel in the dark whether they are entering the right staircase' - Lutyens intimated that the College could not afford any lighting.

The 19th century nevertheless brought a remarkable array of worthies to the College starting with Sir Samuel Morland the inventor of the speaking trumpet, the pump and the calculating machine, the Marquess of Queensbury, formulator of the Boxing rules and persecutor of Oscar Wilde, Charles Stewart Parnell the Irish Nationalist leader and Charles Kingsley the writer.

Parnell came up in 1865 and was given ground floor rooms because of his sleepwalking. He was involved in a fight with a townsman, was sued, fined twenty guineas and then sent down. A different reason given for his being sent down is that he fell in love with a pretty girl called Daisy whom he would meet by the river - against all the rules, of course. He wanted to marry her but could not possibly do so and they continued to meet secretly by the river. One day as he came up to meet her, he found that Daisy had drowned whilst waiting for him, an inquest was held and Parnell had to give evidence and was sent down as a result of his involvement.

Charles Kingsley, clergyman and novelist, came up in 1838 and spent most of his time escaping the College by going over the walls at forbidden hours to inspect 'the glories of the world'... and to go fishing. He was not that simple; during an examination, for example, he was asked to describe a 'common pump' whereupon he drew a picture of a pump in a village with a church, women and children and a little notice next to the pump saying 'this pump is locked during divine service'. The other students must have loved him.

The 20th century saw the arrival in 1923 of Lord Burghley, the Olympic medallist in 1928 and 1932 (depicted in the film 'Chariots of Fire'). A.E Benson was Master from 1915 to 1925, the writer of the words of 'Land of Hope and Glory', a great benefactor to the College but a rather egotistical man whose coat of arms or initials appear at least 18 times on College buildings. Another student of the College who became a great

British symbol was George L. Mallory who died a few feet from the summit of Mount Everest in 1924 and who wanted to climb it 'because it was there'.

Magdalene was the last college in Cambridge to admit females in 1988. At the beginning of that fateful term, the male students wore black armbands in mourning whilst parading a coffin and the College flag was flown at half mast....

*   *   *

Generally, the arrival of women students caused concern; there were debates as to 'whether sexual equality at Cambridge involves the ruin of civilization' and Li Hung Chang, asked to comment on the new women's colleges, Girton and Newnham, simply said: 'Too Muchee Girlee!'

PEMBROKE COLLEGE

In the forlorn hope that French and English students would learn to live in peace, the French Lady Marie St Pol de Valence, Countess of Pembroke founded 'The Hall of Marie Valence' in 1347. It later became known as Pembroke Hall and only in 1856 as Pembroke College. Enough of dry history ....

Poor young Marie was only 17 when she married the Earl of Pembroke who was 50. The old boy decided to enter a joust during the wedding celebrations and was killed accidentally so that it was said that Marie was 'maid, wife and widow in one day'. She survived him 42 years and died 'full of days and good deeds'.

Marie also founded Denney Abbey near Cambridge and she 'enjoined her Fellows at Cambridge to visit the nuns to give ghostly counsel on just occasion'. Whatever that meant, it is reported that the Fellows were 'not wanting in their courteous and conscientious addresses unto them', and one can guess at what went on.

The Countess also built the first private chapel in Cambridge, now the

Old Library, which was subsequently decorated with a beautiful plaster ceiling depicting the undersides of birds as they fly, a sight that can for once be enjoyed in total safety. In the 17th century Matthew Wren, once a Fellow here, commissioned from his nephew a new chapel as a result of a vow he had made: if he should ever be released from the Tower of London wherein Oliver Cromwell had imprisoned him, he would build a great chapel in his old college. Wren was released after over 10 years and the resulting chapel is Christopher Wren's first completed work.

Back to the 16th century, when Pembroke was the temporary home of numerous famous people. Firstly, there was Nicholas Ridley, Master in 1540, one of the Bishops burned at the stake in Oxford by Queen Mary. Then Edmund Spenser, the poet who was here from 1569; he was always ill and pecuniary allowances were made to him on account of his illnesses: 'Spenser, ill for 4 weeks 6s 8d; 2 weeks 3 s 4d.' Maybe it was worth it. He eventually became so popular with Elizabeth I that she granted him a pension of £50 a year, hopefully without having to be ill.

There was also Lancelot Andrews, Master in 1589, one of the translators of James I's Bible. Andrews was said to be acquainted with so many languages that 'had he lived at the time he might have served as Translator-General at the confusion of tongues'. He had perhaps been impressed by Elizabeth I's visit to Pembroke in 1566 when she said: 'Ah! Domus antiqua et religiosa' when she could simply have said 'Ah! Ancient and religious house.' Lastly, Gabriel Harvey, writer and friend of Spenser was also at Pembroke. He had a running battle of insults with Thomas Nashe, wit and dramatist, who was at St John's College. Nashe wrote that Harvey was 'distractedly enamoured of his own beauty' and walked 'holding his gown up to his middle, that the wenches may see what a fine leg and dainty foot he hath'. If you have got it, flaunt it.

Samuel Hassnett was Master from 1605 and Bishop of Chichester at the same time. He was seldom at College and was extremely unpopular when he did visit. All the College linen, used only on special occasions, was ruined by him and his retinue: 'ye college napery of very fayre diaper and damaske is extremely worn and spoyled ... his men have most negligently stained it and wiped their shoes with it.' Arguments on his lack of manners and hygiene were followed by more arguments and the Fellows eventually appealed to the King to kick him out.

The 18th century saw the arrival of William Pitt, probably Pembroke's most famous student. He came to the College in 1773 when 14 years old accompanied by his nurse; he became a Member of Parliament at 18, Chancellor of the Exchequer at 22 and Prime Minister at 24! They no longer make them like that and as a monument to him after his death the Pitt Press was built opposite the College - it looks like a church because of its Gothic architecture and, over the years, it has become known as the Freshers' Church as a result of new, 'fresh' students being tricked by older students into going to attend a service there on the first Sunday of their residence.

The other famous resident of Pembroke in the 18th century was the poet Thomas Gray who had fled from Peterhouse and lived here until his death in 1771. He had rooms overlooking the beautiful Fellows' and Master's gardens and was diverted from his constant melancholic moods by the activities of the eccentric Master Roger Long. Master Long was a wit, author, scientist and amateur mechanic who built a working model of the solar system which could accommodate 30 people sitting in it whilst it revolved. Long also installed a private printing press in the Master's lodge and invented 'a water-velocipede with which he would divert himself on a sheet of water in his garden' in view and to the rare amusement of Thomas Gray.

Serious Gray, who wrote 'Cambridge is very ugly, she is very dirty, and very dull' and who died at the age of 55, should have learnt the lesson about having fun in life from the not so dull Roger Long who became Vice-Chancellor at the age of 89.

In the 19th century, the famous architect Alfred Waterhouse came to the College and persuaded the Fellows that the Hall was so rotten it was unsafe and needed to be pulled down. The gullible Fellows agreed whereupon Waterhouse actually had to use gunpowder to demolish the unyielding structure before building a new Hall. In Pembroke's case, the spirit was weak but the flesh more than willing to resist ...

PETERHOUSE COLLEGE

The oldest College in Cambridge, Peterhouse was founded in 1284 by Hugh de Balsham, Bishop of Ely, for a Master and 14 'worthy but impoverished Fellows'. The Fellows were scholars and teachers who were expected to live in but teach outside the College an who were to be 'studiously engaged in the pursuit of literature'; for mutual encouragement (truthfully, because of poverty) several Fellows had to share the same room, only the Master had his own, and in order to minimise distractions, the statutes insisted that no washerwomen were allowed in the rooms, especially young ones...

Apart from fighting off the usual Peasants' revolts and ever present plagues, Peterhouse yielded no reports of major events nor of oddfellows nor funny tales for almost three hundred years. Then came Dr Andrew Perne, Master from 1554 to 1589. Edmond Spencer and his friend Gabriel Harvey thought him an unsavoury character and described him in a remarkable character assassination as 'a busy and dizzy head, a brazen forehead, a leaden brain, a wooden unit, a copper face, a stony breast... a morning book worm and afternoon malt worm, a right juggler as full of his sleights, wiles, odd shifts and knavish practises as his skin can hold!' However, it was thanks to his peculiar qualities that Dr Perne was able to pilot his College astutely through very troubled times by tailoring his religious views to match whatever was the order of the day. His initials were said to stand for 'A Puritan, A Papist and A Puritan in turn' as he started as Protestant Chaplain to Edward VI, he became Catholic Dean of Ely under Mary Tudor and renounced the Pope for Elizabeth I!

In the 17th century, there was more trouble. Matthew Wren, the uncle of Sir Christopher Wren, was Master in 1628 and built a new chapel and library. When the Parliamentarians won the Civil War, they imprisoned Wren and destroyed 100 cherubim and angels and broke most of the windows in the chapel. He must have wished Dr Perne was still in charge. Wren is probably responsible for the King thinking he ruled by Divine Right, and therefore responsible for the Civil War, as he had once told James I that his dogs 'hunted not by common law, but by prerogative'. James was delighted.

The poet Thomas Gray (of 'Elegy written in a Country Churchyard' fame) came up to Peterhouse in 1734 but hated it and moved to Pembroke after less than a year. He was constantly teased by the other students and disapproved of all the noise they made. Gray was terrified of fire and had asked for a 36 foot rope to be attached to an iron bar below his window so that he could escape easily should the need arise. Lord Percival, a fellow student, organised one night for a small fire to be started in Gray's staircase. Gray saw the smoke and smelt the fire, hurried to his window and, the story goes, he dashed down the rope all the way into a waiting tub of cold water, dressed only in a nightgown and a 'delicate white nightcap'. After that, he left for Pembroke.

Some people prospered in the 18th century, such as Henry Cavendish, the scientist. He was the first to measure the density of water and the weight of the earth as being six thousand million million million tons. It has been said that he was a unique figure in the annals of science for two reasons: firstly, when he went to the Royal Society he went to listen rather than to be listened to and secondly, when he died he left over £1 million in his will! There was money in science then ... Cavendish was probably unlucky in love as he was so shy and feared women so much that he could not look at them and could only communicate with them in writing - thank god he had money.

Peterhouse has educated many other scientists including Sir Frank Whittle, the inventor of the jet engine, Sir Christopher Cockerell, the inventor of the hovercraft and Charles Babbage, the inventor of the first mechanical computer. Professor Tait, in the early 19th century, was not so lucky. He demonstrated to his colleagues that 'the laws of physics set a definite limit to the maximum distance possible for a golf ball to travel and he calculated that maximum' only to be disproved almost immediately by an 'impossibly colossal drive' by his own son, Freddie Tait.

There were many changes to the College during the 19th century, some thanks to a great benefactor, William Stone who came in 1875 as a scholar; generosity is probably a good idea to achieve longevity as Stone died in 1958, aged 101. One of the Masters created a deer park but all the deer had died by the 1930's and another Master made Peterhouse the first college to have electricity, which resulted in complaints from the laundresses in nearby 'Laundress Green' about the dirt which emanated from the generators (working on coal at the time).

Francis Barnes, Master until 1838 and the last man to wear a wig in Cambridge, was of the school of Dr Perne. It was the time of the Election of the Chair of Moral Philosophy for the University, a prestigious post for which by statutes the electors are the Master of Peterhouse, the Vice-Chancellor and two professors of Divinity. In case of a stalemate, the Master of Peterhouse has the casting vote. Since Barnes was Vice-Chancellor at the time, he elected himself on behalf of the Master of Peterhouse and of the Vice-Chancellor and since this led to a tie against the two professors, he used his casting vote to win the election.

The prize, however, belongs to Bishop Keene of Chester, Master of the College in the 18th century. Sir Robert Walpole, then Prime Minister, offered Keene a 'rich living' on condition that he married one of Walpole's natural daughters. Keene jilted the daughter having accepted the living but 'kept the peace' by giving her £600 per annum out of it!

The last word goes to the Peterhouse student sitting for his examination in Biblical history. He was certainly not one of those students about

WITH THIS MONEY,
I THEE JILT

whom it was said that 'they worked so hard, they will never come to any good in later life'. He was asked which were the major and which the minor prophets. He did not know the answer and so he replied that 'he refused to draw invidious distinctions between these truly great men'.

QUEENS' COLLEGE

It was actually Rector Andrew Dokett who founded the College in 1446 as 'Saint Bernard's College' for a President, as opposed to the usual Master, and four Fellows. His fame and probably his money only lasted two years when Margaret of Anjou, Henry's VI's wife, refounded the College as 'The Queen's College of Saint Margaret and Saint Bernard' in order 'to laud and honneure of sexe feminine'. The Queen was well connected and her coat of arms shows her claim to the kingdoms and duchies of Austria-Hungary, Naples, Jerusalem, Bar, Anjou and Lorraine. The College's good connections continued with a second Queen, Elizabeth of Woodville, wife of Edward IV, becoming its patroness, hence the College becoming 'Queens' College'. Later, it was even enriched by Richard III who gave the College lands that did not belong to him!

The greatest member of the College in the 16th century, arguably of all time, was Erasmus, the Dutch scholar and philosopher. He was brought to Queens' by John Fisher, President of the College and Bishop of Rochester, the same John Fisher who did so much for several colleges at Cambridge and who was beheaded by Henry VIII for denying the King's supremacy.

Erasmus taught Greek in Cambridge from 1510 to 1514 and is credited with making Cambridge the foremost university after being second for so long to Oxford. But he seemed to have been a whinger and a pain in the neck.... He was definitely not happy living in Cambridge and constantly complained about the climate, the food and the drink (typical foreigner). Erasmus hated the College ale, which he called 'raw, small and windy' and he hated the locals; 'Cambridge townsmen go beyond the inhospitable Britons, who have malice joined with their clownishness' but he found the women 'the kissing kind' (untypical foreigner) so perhaps Margaret of Anjou had succeeded in her aims. Erasmus grumbled that the burning of heretics was putting up the price of firewood and contributing to the high costs of life in Cambridge and he 'worked off his spleen riding with a fierce countenance round and round the market place on horseback'.

Mind you, he had some cause: having found that the College wine was also no better than vinegar, Erasmus ordered a barrel of choice wine to be sent to him by a friend. On arrival, he found that the carters had drunk it all on the way, leaving him 'only the scent of it'. A second barrel arrived half filled with water which Erasmus blamed for giving him an attack of shingles...

Later in the century, the confirmed bachelor Chaderton, became President in 1568. Chaderton gave an outrageous sermon on matrimony at a wedding he was conducting. He said 'that the choice of a wife is full of hazards, not unlike as if one in a barrel full of serpents should grope for one fish; if he escapes harm of the snakes and lights on a fish, he may be thought fortunate, yet let him not boast, for perhaps it may be but an eel'. This man, full of charm and tact, eventually got married himself.

Another charmer, a student at Queens' years later, was known as Old Creevey. Creevey had no conspicuous talent and no money but succeeded in living the whole of his life at the cost of others. He led a vagrant life, visiting people, carrying with him no possessions and having no creditors. He was felt to be totally harmless and was known as the only man in society who posessed nothing but knew everyone and everything... He was, surely, far from a fool.

Dr Edward Martin, President in the 17th century, was not too bothered about possessions either; together with other Masters, he sent a large shipment of College silver to help the King during the Civil War. The shipment was smuggled past Cromwell and his men, waiting in ambush, but cost the Masters their freedom when victorious Cromwell imprisoned them in the Tower of London and nearly sold them into slavery in Algiers which even Old Creevey would not have enjoyed.

The 18th century saw the arrival of two very odd characters, Ferdinand Smythies, a Fellow, and John Lloyd, a scholar. Smythies was a great glutton and on one occasion, walking with a friend, he came upon 'a woman with a child in her arms, a fine boy, fresh and white haired'. He cried out to his friend in the mother's hearing: 'Good God, how nicely that boy would eat, boiled with colly flowers.'

SWEET CHILD....
ESPECIALLY WITH COLLY FLOWERS

Lloyd was even more uncouth. He once hurled a chair out of his window onto a passing carriage in the street below; when the passengers sent a servant up to investigate, Lloyd beat him up and threw him into mudflats adjoining the river. Then the driver of the carriage came up to see what had happened to the first man and was himself beaten up. In an effort to show that it did not condone such unprovoked abuse, the College forced Lloyd to apologise to his victims and made him learn a Cicero Oration!

Isaac Milner became President in the early 1800's. Milner was asked by visitors what relic of Erasmus the College might own. He replied 'nothing except a huge corkscrew.... and I am afraid there was nothing in his principles to keep him from making very assiduous use of it', so presumably Erasmus finally found something worth opening and drinking. Milner was no saint himself, being coarse and loud and enormously fat. He was also Dean in Carlisle and stayed there two years after going up for a 'brief' visit in 1814 - students unscrewed the brass knocker from his lodge door and sent it up to him in Carlisle with the message that 'perhaps it might be of some use to the Dean of Carlisle, for it was of no use in Cambridge'.

Not everybody objected to unauthorised absenteeism from the College. On receiving a complaint about his son, a father answered the latter's tutor in the mid 1800's: 'I do not understand the tenor of your communication. When I was an undergraduate at Queens' it would have been accounted a disgrace to the College if any man had been present in Hall on Newmarket race day.'

Queens' College boasts two outstanding architectural features. Firstly, the dial dating from 1733 which is one of the finest sundials in Britain and one of the few moondials in the world. Secondly, the wooden mathematical bridge, originally built in 1749 and rebuilt in 1904, known by that name because people believed it was built with no nails or screws.

The bridge leads to the Dokett building, erected in 1912 and which incorporated the first purpose-built baths. This opulence led to the exclamation by an elderly don that the baths were an unnecessary extravagance since the students only lived at the College eight weeks at a time ...

ST CATHARINE'S COLLEGE

As the wheel in the College coat of arms illustrates, this College is named after Saint Catharine of Alexandria who was crucified on a wheel - the Catharine wheel fireworks are also called after her. The College was founded in 1473 by Robert Woodlark, the third Provost of King's College, as Katharine Hall, for one Master and three Fellows to study philosophy and sacred theology and to pray for the souls of their benefactors ever after. It became St Catharine's College in 1860.

Woodlark, like several other founders, gave the College little money but all his books for the library, with strict conditions: the books had to be examined annually and could only be taken out for repairs; visitors had to leave the library by sunset whilst the Fellows could keep on working by candlelight. What a lark.

The beginning was difficult, with no students at all for the first 100 years and so little money, and therefore such a low standard of living, that even Government officials refused to stay for free at the College! In the 1575 agreement between the Town and the University for fighting fires, whereas other colleges had to provide four water buckets, St Catharine's only had to provide two ...

Lucky Dr Sandys was Master in the 16th century when the powerful Duke of Northumberland came for a visit to Cambridge accompanied by a small army. The Duke had declared his allegiance to Lady Jane Grey on Edward VI's death and insisted that Dr Sandys should give a sermon in support. Dr Sandys, not too keen on showing his support for a seemingly lost cause but terrified of upsetting the Duke, gave a sermon based on a quotation he happened to alight on by chance the previous night in his Bible: 'And they answered Joshua, saying, all that thou commandest us, we will do; and whithersoever thou sendest us, we will go.' (Joshua 1.16). Sandys' tact and luck saved the day. But then the Duke of Northumberland changed his allegiance and announced his support for Queen Mary ... On hearing the joyful ringing of bells, Dr Sandys went to take his seat as Vice-Chancellor in the Regent House where he was immediately assaulted by Papists who tried to evict him: meeting violence with violence 'the Doctor, being a man of metal, groped for his dagger, and probably had despatched some of them, had not Dr Bill and Dr Blythe, by their prayers and entreaties, persuaded him to patience'. Sandys survived a while longer but his luck eventually ran out, he was evicted from the University, imprisoned in London but managed to escape overseas: his Mastership and four notable geldings were confiscated!

The 17th century was definitely the period of the good, the bad and the strange for the College.

Firstly there was the false generosity of John Hills, Master in 1623. At a time when the College was still very poor, Hills declared out of his love and affection for his College 'to release it from all sums and duties whatsoever due or hereafter to become due to him from the College for any cause whatsoever from the beginning of the world'. A magnificent offer, but when he was investigated after various accusations, it was found that Hills actually owed the College £68 (a huge sum at the time) together with silver plate which had disappeared from the Master's lodge. His successor Richard Sibbs 'found the house in a mean condition' but improved the College so much that he inspired the couplet:

Of this blest man let just praise be given
Heaven was in him before he was in Heaven.

A worthwhile gift received by the College from an ex-student was the Bull Inn given by Dr Gostlin, then Master of Gonville and Caius. Not a laudable act as far as the students of Caius were concerned and they would drink to the confusion to the memory of Dr Gosling 'who was such a Goose as to leave the Bull to Catharine'. A little later, John Addenbrooke, who had been a student in 1697, left his money at his death in 1719, approximately £4500, to found the famous Addenbrooke Hospital in Cambridge

Still in the 17th century, St Catharine's welcomed as students, William Wotton, probably the youngest undergraduate ever, and James Shirley who became known as the last of the Elizabethan authors. Wotton was born in 1666, had learned Latin, Greek and Hebrew by the age of six, Arabic and Syriac by the age of seven, had entered St Catharine's when nine years old and was just twelve when he took his degree. He then learned Anglo Saxon and Welsh and became a Fellow of the Royal Society at twenty one ... James Shirley was in favour under the Stewarts, kept his plays going under the Parliamentarians and survived the revenge of the Stewarts at the Restoration only to die with his wife as a result of exposure and shock after the Great Fire of London in 1666.

Two unpopular fellows were John Eachard, Master from 1670, and Lowther Yates. Eachard had been unwise enough to complain that there was too much Latin content in the University curriculum and was called as a result 'a Rebel, Traitor, Scot, Sadducee and Socinian ... a Barbarian, Indian, Turk and Jew'! Lowther Yates was supposed to be 'a square fat man mainly memorable for being the victim of a rude nephew who, on seeing him in trousers rather than shorts and stockings, cried out: 'Gadzoons, Gadzoons, Lowther Yates in Pantaloons!' One can only thank St Catharine's for teaching the world several new words and insults.

Then came the athletic and energetic Joseph Proctor. A very popular man, he was elected for the third time Vice-Chancellor when he was already very old; Proctor jumped on his horse and galloped 70 miles from Norwich where he lived to state his view that he was too old and frail for the job and then galloped straight back to Norwich again!

Proctor was obviously not riding one of Thomas Hobson's horses. Hobson owned livery stables in the late 17th century where the present chapel stands. Whenever a customer required to hire a horse, he was forced to take by strict rotation the horse which had been longest at rest in the stables. Hobson would reply to any complaints 'my choice or no choice', hence the expression 'Hobson's choice'.

The matter of 'choice' came up again in 1861 during the elections for the Mastership. Two Fellows, Robinson and Jameson, had reached the finals with an equal number of votes each, with only their own votes left to cast: courtesy and etiquette required each man to vote for the other and so Jameson politely voted for Robinson. Robinson, however, was desperate to get married which only the Master of the College could do in those days, so he voted for himself and was therefore elected by a majority of one! Jameson never forgave him nor did many others but Robinson, the cad, was long lived and remained Master for nearly 50 years until his death in 1909.

*　　*　　*

In more recent years, a don who believed himself to be crafty gave a stone to a prospective student as an admission test and told him to throw it out of the window in his own individual way. The student immediately threw the stone, without opening the window, through the pane of glass....

ST JOHN'S COLLEGE

Bishop John Fisher, the Cambridge stalwart, once again persuaded Lady Margaret Beaufort, Henry VII's mother, to found a college on the site of a 13th century hospital run by the monks of St John: the Charter of the 'College of St John the Evangelist' was granted on the 9th April 1511.

At the start, accommodation was far from lavish with the statutes insisting that each Fellow should have his pupils studying and sleeping in his rooms, 'not more than two to a bed, unless they be under 14'. This was a deliberate attempt to encourage the older members 'to advise their younger chambermates, show them a good example and instruct them in discipline'. Discipline was no doubt exercised by everyone.

ARE YOU SURE YOU'RE UNDER 14?

The day started when the bell rang at 4am followed by mass before 6am, two more hours of lectures and then food. Free time followed until 3pm when there were two more hours of lectures followed by supper. Students were not allowed to leave the College without the Master's permission and Fellows had to be back by 8pm when the gate was closed. Speaking English instead of Classical languages resulted in fines such as bread and water only at meals, or even a whipping.

Winters too must have been fun as Dr Leaver wrote in 1550 that members of the College could not keep warm and had 'to run up and down half an hour to get heat in their feet when they go to bed'; he also said that for dinner they made do with 'a penny piece of beef among four'. It is not surprising that Hugh Ashton, one of the first Fellows, who died in 1522, is depicted twice on his tomb, on the top dressed in his academic robes and below as an emaciated corpse in a shroud.

More funds did reach the College when Mary Cavendish, Countess of Shrewsbury finally sorted out her family relationships (she married the heir to the Earl of Shrewsbury on the same day as her mother, Bess of Hardwick, married the Earl) and her relationship with the King whom she hated and who imprisoned her in 1611 and 1618.

Most of the students of the College, however, remained poor for a very long time and were laughed at by those of other colleges for having no money. One story was told of a St John's man who had invited eleven friends for dinner, at the end of which he passed round one bottle of port and said with a noble air: 'Not one of you men shall leave this room until that bottle is empty.'

The best known member of the College in the 16th century was William Cecil, Lord Burghley, who became Elizabeth I's famous principal officer of state. He was Chancellor of the University from 1559 to 1598 and made 'Cambridge better known than Oxford' - some at that other University might disagree. Robert Greene, the dramatist, was here before moving on to Clare College. He died in his early thirties after leading a dissipated life and wrote on his deathbed: 'Being at the University I light myself amongst wags as lewd as myself, with whom I consumed the flower of my youth, who drew me to travel into Italy and Spain, in which places I saw and practised such villainy as it is abominable to declare.' Modern day travellers, we are told, need still beware..... Then there was Dr Whittaker, the Master hated by his Fellows whom he accused of poor judgement in that they would always choose to elect to a Fellowship a religious dunce rather than a learned rakehell. It must be remembered that most Fellows were clerics (and not allowed to marry until 1882) but Whittaker maintained that their choice was wrong as 'religion can always be counterfeited by a religious dunce whilst a rakehell could be seen to improve unto temperance'.

St John's suffered like all the royalist colleges during the Civil War with its Master Dr Beale arrested by Cromwell for sending the College silver to help the King; the great Lord Protector even considered sending the good Doctor to Algiers for sale as a slave to the highest bidder. The linenfold doors of the Gate Tower were battered but survived a seige by Cromwell's troops and were restored in 1666; the College still celebrates the Restoration of the Monarchy on the 29th May with a feast in the Hall.

These were difficult and sometimes silly times, perhaps why a student of the College, Francis Lord Guildford thought it safer to write on subjects such as 'The Gravitation of Fluids contained in the Bladders of

Fishes' whilst Dr Jenkin, a Master of the time, refused to put up with the airs and graces of one of his Fellows, Matt Prior, the poet and diplomat who had become ambassador to Paris. 'Dr Jenkin', it was said, 'knew his own dignity too well to suffer a Fellow of his College to sit down in his presence.' So there.

The 18th century was safer and more comfortable with the usual exceptions. Even towards the end of the century there was great poverty among some students such as James Wood, mathematician; when he first came up he lived in a garret at the top of a turret with no money for light or heat, and so to study he would sit on the steps below the feeble staircase light with his feet wrapped in straw, but his endeavours were rewarded as he eventually became Master.

Wood's ghost, said to be haunting that staircase, is one of the several ghosts who originated the 18th century at St John's: there is the ghost who appeared in 1706 to a tutor Robert Grave whilst away on a trip, warning him of the impending death of another tutor Arthur Orchard, and Orchard was indeed found dead by Grove on his return to St John's. Other ghosts, moaning and groaning from a house situated opposite the College, were 'exorcised' by four Fellows 'threatening to discharge their pistols' in their direction. John Edwards, a more sensible Fellow, complained that 'among the university men almost half of them are disordered in their brains'...

William Wilberforce, who helped to abolish the slave trade, came up in 1776. He was told by his tutor that since he had money he should not trouble himself with books and so Wilberforce kept a great Yorkshire pie in his room to share with all his visitors and he spent his time singing and playing cards. Then came in 1787 the better known William, Wordsworth, who lived in F staircase in rooms he described as gloomy. They cannot have been that urban and gloomy since only ten years before a hunted stag was killed in the doorway of G staircase, which seems rather rural. Wordsworth was not generally impressed by St

John's. He described the Fellows as 'men unscoured, grotesque in character, tricked out like aged trees' and, like Wilberforce, he enjoyed 'the benefits to be derived from the neglect of his teachers' and concentrated on enjoying a good social life, happy in the companionship of his fellow youths and he loved idleness, a pastime totally unappreciated by most students.

Architecture and buildings play an important part in the humorous history of the College.

WISH HE'L
SING BEFOR
THE PIE

Among the unusual must be listed the carving of the coat of arms of Lady Margaret Beaufort above the Gate Tower entrance with its curious mythical beasts whose horns supposedly swivel back to front; the Fellows' panelled Combination room, the longest room in Cambridge at 93 ft and still only lit by candlelight, where part of the D-Day landings were planned and the 'Wedding Cake' central tower which has no clock face. The story goes that Trinity College was building a clock tower at the same time and since the colleges wisely refused to have conflicting chimes, a race was agreed with the first to finish its tower allowed to install a clock.... Trinity won and its clock now chimes twice, once for St John's. Yet another story tells of the students who climbed St John's tower and painted such a realistic clock face on one of the blank stone circles that the Master, noticing the clock, sent for the porter to tell him it had stopped! The porter, the tale continues, sent a man up the tower to repair the clock...

In 1831, the 'Bridge of Sighs' was built, linking the College to new buildings across the river; the difference with its Venetian namesake is that the bridge has bars and tracery to stop students coming 'in' (late at night) as opposed to escaping from an unpleasant fate. In 1956, students punted a small car up the river and hung it from the bridge which must have sighed with resignation.

The chapel was designed in 1869 by Sir Gilbert Scott and it was said that his original plans were confused with those of St Pancras Station in London. His design incorporated a spire but an Old Johnian, Henry Hoare, gave £3,000 and promised another £1,000 annually for five years to build a tower instead; he died after two years in a railway accident and the College had to fund the remainder. Activities on the Tower are usually restricted to the chapel choir singing hymns from its roof every Ascension Day at noon, until one day in 1932 when a student performed his own ascension and placed a surplice over one of the not too easily accessible statues. A rather portly porter agreed to be lowered on a rope from a window above and succeeded in removing the offending article whereupon he was found too heavy to haul back up again; he was left to swing gently in the breeze until a longer rope was found and he was lowered directly to the ground.

The College boat club is called the Lady Margaret Boat Club, as opposed to St John's Boat Club, supposedly as a result of a very unpleasant event. During May Bumps, races during which a boat is supposed to bump the one in front, the crew of a St John's boat placed a sword, as a joke, sticking out at the front of the boat and it allegedly killed the Cox of Trinity College's second boat during a bump. As a result, Trinity College only ran a first and a third boat as a mark of respect and St John's was banned from races in its name for 100 years. The Lady Margaret Boat Club dates from 1825, its oarsmen wear scarlet jackets which gave rise to the name 'Blazer' and it first challenged Oxford to a boat race in 1829 on the neutral River Thames in London.

Lastly, worthies of the College include Lord Palmerston, 19th century Prime Minister, John Couch Adams also here in the 1800's whose youthful vow to account for irregularities in the orbit of Uranus led him to discover the planet Neptune (he also presided over the decision that the zero meridian should pass through Greenwich), the well named George Downing Liveing, Professor of Chemistry in the 1920's, who died run down by a bicycle at the age of 97, and Bishop Colenso...

Colenso's name reputedly made 'the loudest noise in the world' in his time and he was hated for disproving 'arithmetical inconsistencies' in the Pentateuch (Old Testament books). After studying at St John's in the mid 1800's, he became a missionary bishop in Africa, which occupation he happily pursued until he was confronted one day by 'the famous Zulu whose awkward questions gave him food for thought'.

The Zulu, it seems, refused to believe the facts and figures given him from the Bible's Pentateuch and so the good bishop went through the figures 'in the spirit of a chartered accountant' and demonstrated to the educated world that the Zulu was right, as Colenso calculated that according to the Bible:

1. There were 42 boys in every Hebrew family.

2. Moses' mother was at least 256 years old when he was born.

3. 603,350 warriors assembled in a court where 5000 at most could fit.

4. During the Second Passover, priests sacrificed 50,000 lambs at the rate of 400 per minute.

Colenso's superior, a Bishop Gray of Cape Town, instead of applauding his prowess at arithmetics, sacked him...

SIDNEY SUSSEX COLLEGE

Her executors having bribed Elizabeth I to grant a royal licence, the College of Lady Francis Sidney, Countess of Sussex, was founded immediately upon her death in 1589 with the endowment of £5000 and all her silver plate. She wanted it to be called 'The Ladie Ffrauncis Sydney Sussex Colledge'; Lady Francis was childless, with quaint ideas of spelling, but she said that 'such learned persons who receive their Breeding in her Foundation may be termed her Issue'.

Perhaps the most famous student of the College was, alas, Oliver Cromwell, the great Puritan, Parliamentarian and the equal of Henry VIII in the wholesale destruction of buildings.

Cromwell came up to Sidney on the 23rd of April 1616, the day Shakespeare died. Thomas Carlyle, the 19th century writer, described that day: on the one hand, one could imagine Anne Hathaway weeping over Shakespeare's bed in Stratford, the witness to the end of great literature whilst on the other, Cromwell's arrival at Cambridge heralded 'the beginning, so to speak, of armed Puritanism - the armed appeal of Puritanism to the invisible God of Heaven against the many very visible (to Cromwell of course) devils on earth'.

Cromwell spent more time playing sports at Cambridge, especially football, rather than studying. Football, however, was not well thought of at the time, being 'fitter for clowns than for scholars ... to excel in it a man must be a good boxer, runner and wrestler'. The same can surely be said today. Our Puritan regretted his favourite pastime in his later years and wrote about his wasted hours playing football: 'Ah, I have lived in and loved darkness and hated light; I was a chief, a chief of sinners.' He actually only sinned briefly as he had to leave Cambridge after one year to support his family after his father's death.

OYER 'ERE SON...
ON ME ROUNDHEAD!

During the Civil War, the sympathies of the College were not with the Parliamentarians and the Master was imprisoned by unforgiving Cromwell for sending £100 to help the King's cause.

At the Restoration, Cromwell's body was exhumed, hanged and beheaded. His head was impaled on a pole outside Westminster Hall; it blew down during a great storm twenty years later but it took almost three hundred years before the College, more forgiving than Cromwell, inherited the skull and buried it secretly in the antechapel in 1960.

Still not too popular, Cromwell's portrait in the dining hall is usually covered out of tact during visits by members of the Royal Family.

Battling for a totally different team, Walter Montague was a student here; he was a 'devout Popish author' who could have become a short lived English Bishop under Catholic Mary but instead had the wisdom to emigrate and he died in 1669 as a French Abbot. A second well known author of the time and once a student at Sidney was Thomas Fuller from whose books many stories and quotes have found their way into this humble effort.

Thomas May, Fellow in 1609 and historian to Charles I, was perhaps a less gifted author. When he was turned down for the position of Poet Laureate by the Royalists, he went over to the Puritans and became one of the 'Secretaries for the Parliament'. May died a few years later from 'tying his nightcap too close under his fat chin and cheeks'. Not a pretty sight.

Another literary ex-student, albeit gifted this time and who came a few centuries later, was Sir Robert L'Estrange, the editor of 'The Public Intelligencer', the first English newspaper.

Towards the end of the 17th century, after the Restoration, the College became a little more riotous. A certain William Butler was sent down because 'he distempered himself with drink and committed outrageous

96

insolences against the Dean in breaking his window with brickbats', three other students were expelled for attempted burglary of the Master's lodge - they had tried to cut a hole in the door - and in 1669 William Bach was also expelled for 'with his sword and pistol threatening some of the Fellows and assaulting others'.

Studies were not always taken seriously. In the late 18th century, Weedon Butler, a student who reckoned that the study of mathematics in particular was unhealthy, wrote his disapproval to his father:

'It was remarked in the Senate House (for the examination) that I had more the appearance of an idle lounger than of a candidate for Academical Honours. Indeed I could scarcely avoid being of the same opinion when I beheld the ghastly looks of my competitors. One of them fainted away on the first morning of the Examination; several declined the contest from mere debility; and most of those who did endure to the end looked more like worn-out rakes than men under three-and-twenty in the bloom of youth and in the prime of manhood.' He was probably making excuses for failing but his views were well supported, especially when a Henry Kirke White of St John's College died prematurely 'as the innocent victim of higher mathematics' in the opinion of many!

The 19th century was a period of decline. Food was short as is illustrated by the story of the Fellow A.A Vasinart who was 'moved to buy a healthy young donkey' which he fattened on oil cake and had killed ready for eating; the latter action was 'warmly taken up by another Fellow, Hardy' under whose direction 'every part of the animal was utilised'. The meat was apparently 'delicious, rather like swan' but not everybody approved of these Chinese style culinary discoveries: 'among the lower orders the proceedings excited the greatest possible disgust, so much so that the man who usually bought the drippings out of the Sidney Sussex kitchen refused to take any that week.'

There were few students at the time, probably because of the food, and the College had to take its boat out of the annual races in 1849 'owing to most of the men taking their degree'. The timing must have been better in 1857 because Sidney not only managed to crew a boat but actually came seventh in the inter-college races despite having only ten students in the whole College! Whereupon the usual Cambridge wit wrote:

> *' There were eight to row and one to steer,*
> *And one to run on the bank and cheer.'*

Some learning did take place as was proved by Archbishop Mackray, a student here in the mid 19th century. Mackray was Bishop of Rupert's Land in Winnipeg, Canada, during the difficult time of the Red River Rebellion; his wise counsels of moderation helped to prevent a massacre and saved lives, and he corresponded with the Colonial authorities in cypher based upon the Latin Grace said before every meal at his old College! It was said that 'it is probably the only occasion on which the College Grace has served the cause of British Expansion'. Latin and religion finally came in useful.

TRINITY COLLEGE

Having succeeded in destroying countless places of learning, Henry VIII decided to redeem himself towards the end of his life; he founded 'The College of the Holy and Undivided Trinity' in 1546 and died five weeks later. Henry wanted his college to be the biggest and the best; he combined previous foundations, including one created by Edward III in the 14th century, gave Trinity massive endowments from dissolved monasteries and certainly succeeded in creating the biggest and the wealthiest College in Cambridge. The Master of the College is to this day appointed by the Crown. Henry now stands by the College gate, carved in stone and holding a wooden chair leg instead of his sceptre, the result of a students' joke in the last century; more recently, as a result of another prank, a toilet brush replaced the chair leg until porters reinstated the statue to its now accepted form with yet another chair leg. Below him are the six shields bearing the coat of arms of Edward III's six sons, the sixth being blank since one of the sons died in infancy before being issued with his own coat of arms.

In 1593, Thomas Nevile, one of the first Masters, was the inspiration behind the enormous Great Court which measures two acres; its 18th century clock strikes the hour twice, the first time with a low note and then with a higher note (the male and female voices in Wordsworth's poem 'Prelude'). There is a tradition that undergraduates try to run around the Great Court while the clock strikes twelve o'clock twice - 380 yards (347.5 metres) in 43 seconds. This tradition was illustrated in the film 'Chariots of Fire': the first recorded victor was the Olympic champion Lord Burghley in 1927 and more recently, Steve Cram and Sebastian Coe succeeded in 1988.

On the intellectual side, the 16th century yielded John Dee, Fellow, who was a 'great mathematician, astronomer, astrologer, cabalist and adept in the occult art'. He was, luckily, acquitted of bewitching Mary Tudor, the Queen, and eventually became a great favourite of Elizabeth I.

In the 17th century, Trinity declined as a result of a series of ill qualified Masters imposed by Charles II and James II. However, Isaac Newton was here in 1661, him of 'an apple fell on my head and proved the laws of gravity to me' fame; a descendant of that same apple tree was planted by the College Gate in 1954. Later on, as a Fellow, he calculated the speed of sound for the first time by stamping his foot in the North Cloister and timing the returning echo.

Poor John North became Master after the Civil War. The Fellows did not like him and made his life a misery. After one last argument, he collapsed in an epileptic fit. His doctors' treatment was to force him to endure continuous noise in order to stay awake .... he died shortly after. He was buried at his request at the entrance to the chapel 'that the

Fellows might trample upon me dead as they have done living'.

A famous character, student and then Master in 1673, was Isaac Barrow. He loved to fight and was 'more addicted to pugilism than study'. His father despaired of him: 'If it should please God to take away any of his children from him, he could best spare Isaac'! On his Grand Tour of Europe, the fashionable pastime of wealthy young men after finishing their studies, Isaac Barrow was in a vessel which was attacked by Algerine pirates. On being posted to a gun, it is said that 'he fought it so valiantly that the pirates retired in disorder'.

Later, back in Cambridge as a Fellow, he was attacked in the street by a huge and savage mastiff ... he seized it by the throat and held it helpless until help arrived. His father would have approved especially as he became an eminent classical and mathematical scholar and a great preacher - although he had the reputation of giving the longest sermons, some lasting up to four hours at which point the vergers would try and drown him with 'organ voluntaries'. Who could therefore blame Sir Christopher Wren for being persuaded by such a man to design the College library for nothing?

One last word about Master Isaac Barrow, Doctor of Divinity: he was at Court and enjoyed this repartee with the Earl of Rochester, an admirer and friend.

Doctor I am yours to the shoe tie.
My Lord I am yours to the ground.
Doctor I am yours to the centre.
My Lord I am yours to the antipodes.
Doctor I am yours to the lowest pit of Hell.
There my Lord I leave you !

In the 18th century, Trinity continued to decline under Richard Bentley, Master from 1700 to 1742. He was again a great scholar but very unpopular as he was difficult and arrogant with masterful methods for collecting money - usually more than the fair share due to him. His misgovernment meant that during this period 'the Fellows drank too much and the students read too little.' His unpopularity started long before he was elected Master, so much so that the Fellows refused to let him through the College gate after his election. Bentley had to climb over a back wall into Trinity quoting the 18th Psalm, 'with the help of God I shall leap over a wall'. The Fellows then tried to oust him after several other arguments but Bentley won in a legal war 'which lasted longer than the siege of Troy'.

His successor William Mansel was not very firm with the students. He got 'very' annoyed with one particular character:
'It is an extraordinary thing that every time I look out of my window you are walking on the grass...'
'It is no less extraordinary' replied the student ' that each time I walk on the grass you are looking out of your window'!

God bless him, he was your typical ineffective schoolmaster type who, on noticing students misbehaving, would simply shout from afar 'I recognise you, gentlemen, I recognise you' and do absolutely nothing.

Discipline was so lax at this time that students, who made the night watchman on King Street drunk on very strong ale and then pitched him and his hut into the river, were simply given 500 lines of Ovid to copy as a punishment. Two odd Fellows were Nicholas Claggett and William Pugh. Claggett was the College librarian from 1706 to 1716 who believed in collecting titles; when he died he was at the same time a Bishop, an Archdeacon, a Prebendary, a Canon and a Rector. William Pugh had written his thesis 'entirely on the covers of letters' and preferred to throw his dirty laundry into the river Cam rather than washing it - he certainly did not follow in Master Bentley's extravagant steps. Pugh lost his job at the University library cataloguing the books because he was discovered reading entire books as opposed to only the title pages. The other Fellows thought him mad but not mad enough to kick out until he was caught in 1790 assaulting a street light with a large stick and shouting 'you are Robespierre' (the French revolutionary leader).

Christopher Wordsworth, the poet's brother, was the Master who tried to make religion compulsory ('compulsory religion is better than no religion'). One tutor at the time asked a student to explain his frequent absences from chapel. The student said that 'he felt no inclination to pray' whereupon the tutor exclaimed: 'I don't want your damned prayers. All that I want is to see your damned face in chapel'!

Eventually, real change came from 1841 under the Mastership of William Whevell. He was double faced, loved by his family and friends and hated by the students for his haughty, arrogant manner. Being the son of a carpenter he probably had a chip on his shoulder. But he was a good scholar and obviously a disciplinarian who made the students work. It is said that he only made one mistake when, as a student, he was trying to win the top academic prize against his arch rival Jacob. He would watch Jacob ride off in the mornings in his hunting gear and thinking his rival was out enjoying himself, Whevell would therefore himself spend the day 'idling'. Jacob meanwhile was going to rooms in a neighbouring village where he would study all day. Jacob, not surprisingly, won the first prize.

Whevell became so haughty with time that a poem was written about him which finished as follows:

> *'You'll find as you tread on the bounds of infinity
> that God's greatest work is the Master of Trinity.'*

The story goes that Whevell was given shelter by a student during a thunderstorm and when the young man tried to converse with him, he replied that 'the Master of the College only talks to students through their tutors'!

Not a man to mess with, Whevell was once woken up at midnight by a cacophony of horns, trumpets, bugles and drums coming from all the surrounding windows with a piano being played in New Court by a student who had already been expelled that day. Whevell tried to open his door which had been tied with rope and finally broke through after three charges. He erupted into New Court where everything was now totally quiet, saw the expelled student standing by his piano, gave a great cry and chased the hapless young man through the colonnades of Nevile's Court and ejected him out of the front gate 'like bad rubbish' ....

W.H Thompson, the Master from 1860 preferred to use sarcasm and wit. At the end of a Fellows' meeting ripe with argument he once said: 'We are none of us infallible, not even the youngest of us.' About another Fellow: 'He talks about pride of intellect; it is a temptation he never experienced.' And about a lazy student: 'All the time that he can spare from the adornment of his person, he devotes to the neglect of his duties' - strangely applicable today also. Finally to a lady who had found 'so much taste' in the writings of a divine preacher who 'gushed and was popular': 'Yes' said Thompson 'so much taste - and all of it bad'!

At this time, a student ready to take Holy Orders asked his tutor, a man called Blakesley:

'Pray, sir, do you think that eternal punishment will consist in moral or physical suffering?' After due hesitation, Blakesley replied: 'I should incline to think moral.'

'Thank you, sir', said the student 'you have no idea what a weight you have lifted from my mind.'

The 19th century saw the likes of Thacheray, Alfred Lord Tennyson and Lord Byron as students at Trinity. Byron started life as he finished it, mostly enjoying himself. In a letter to a friend, he talked of going to parties where there were 'jockies, gamblers, boxers, authors, parsons and poets' not to mention an extraordinary amount of drink. Undergraduates were not allowed to keep dogs so Byron decided to keep a tame bear so that 'it could sit for its Fellowship', a rather direct insult to his tutors! After his death, the College accepted a statue of Byron which had been refused by Westminster Abbey on the grounds of the poet's questionable morals, something not so frowned upon in Cambridge.

This century's pranks started well with William Cole, an infamous hoaxer. In 1905 he impersonated the uncle of the Sultan of Zanzibar, then visiting England, and got the Mayor of Cambridge to lead him and his friends dressed as attendants, on an escorted visit of the town and colleges after which they all lifted up the skirts of their costumes and ran off to waiting cabs. Later, with yet more friends pretending to be workmen, he cordonned off part of Piccadilly and started to dig up the street. Cole finally got into serious trouble when he was caught impersonating the Emperor of Abyssinia on an official visit to HMS Dreadnought.

More serious students of Trinity have included John Dryden, Lord Macaulay the historian, Francis Bacon the philosopher, Vaughan Williams, Lord Rutherford who split the atom in his Cambridge laboratory in 1932, the Prince of Wales here in 1967 and A.A Milne, writer of 'Winnie the Pooh'. All in all, Trinity College has educated two kings, six Prime Ministers of Britain, Nehru, first Prime Minister of India and 28 Nobel Prize winners which is allegedly more than the whole of France!

TRINITY HALL

The College was founded in 1350 by William Bateman, Bishop of Norwich, to replace 700 parish priests who had died of the Black Death which had killed off almost half the population of Britain. It was to educate students in canon and civil law and as a result is still known as the lawyers' College: 'Hall' actually, not 'College' as that name was given by Henry VIII to his own foundation, ignoring the fact there was already a 'Trinity'. Life was rather hard at first and food sparse, for the students at any rate; in the 15th century, one Master wrote 'scholars, like hawks, fly best when sharp, not fully gorged', to which the students answered 'he praised fasting when he was full himself'.

THAT CHICKEN'S SHARPER THAN WE ARE!

Stephen Gardiner was twice Master in the 16th century as well as Bishop of Winchester. He was known as a survivor and called 'naughty divine' as he used all his lawyer's skills first as Lord Chancellor to Henry VIII when he sided against the Pope to support Henry's divorce, making Mary illegitimate, and then when he recanted, supported Mary's claim for legitimacy and became her most powerful statesman.

A little later Thomas Preston, a student at the College, acted in the plays put on to entertain Elizabeth I when she visited the University in 1564. Poor Elizabeth sat through three plays and is said to have given up on the fourth, rather tired, 'for the weakness of the flesh'. However, she thought Preston acted so well and looked so handsome in the play 'Dido' that she tipped him heavily, gave him her royal and virginal hand to kiss and settled an annuity of £20 on him. Preston became Master in 1585 and when Elizabeth gave permission for Masters to marry, he was the first to tie the knot.

A less lucky man was Thomas Tusser who, as a Fellow, had written a book called '500 Points of Good Husbandry'. Believing his own publicity, he left Trinity to run a farm, failed as a farmer and returned penniless to Trinity as a 'servant' in 1574. He was placed in the choir and literally had to sing for his supper.

Trinity Hall certainly owns one of the most interesting libraries with sloped reading desks and valuable books still chained to the shelves below in order to prevent theft. One of the books was written by Erasmus and was published in 1521 by the first printer in Cambridge, the German John Siberch. Siberch had borrowed £20 from the University Chest but ran off home to Germany without paying his debt. His successor, the University Printer repaid the debt of £20 in July 1971 to commemorate the printing of Cambridge's first book - a debt which should have been worth, calculated to have grown at 5% compound per annum, some £69 billion!

I CAN GIVE YOU £20 CASH...
OR A CHEQUE FOR
£69 BILLION...

Two 16th century Trinity Fellows who were apparently keen on roads were Dr Henry Harvey, Master in 1567, and Dr William Mowse. Harvey was for some reason supervising works on a highway when a nobleman saw him and mocked him: 'Doctor, do you think that this highway is the road to heaven?', whereupon Harvey replied: 'Not so, my Lord, for then I think I should not have met you in this place.' Mowse left a bequest in his will for the repairs of highways and as a consequence the first milestones in Britain since the Romans were placed on the London road and bear the College arms.

A different 'builder' was Sir Nathanael Lloyd, an 18th century Master who 'triumphantly flattened' the ceiling in the Hall which was not to his taste but which was 'elevated' again at a later date, showing that time always has its revenge and what comes down must rise again. Then there was a 'gardener', Dr Jowett, a tutor in the late 1700's. He planted a little triangle of shrubbery next to the College in 1793, supposedly to commemorate the beheading of Louis XVI of France. It was deemed rather pathetic and diminutive by some, and the Cambridge wit of the day, Porson, wrote:

> *A little garden little Jowett made*
> *And fenced it with a little palisade;*
> *And when this garden made a little talk*
> *He changed it to a little gravel walk;*
> *If you would know the mind of little Jowett*
> *This little garden don't a little show it.*

People were not generally respectful in those days about making any improvements, however small, to the environment.

The last word for the 18th century must go to Lord Chesterfield who gave his own unique testimonial for the College when he said he liked Trinity Hall because it was smaller than other colleges and only had one clergyman at the time who was also the only College drunkard. He also said that there was little debauchery 'especially among men of standing for the simple reason that one must have the tastes of a street porter to be able to endure it here'!

Things must have changed by the early 19th century. As a student who arrived in 1812, Longueville-Clarke complained that he had been 'cut by almost everyone' because he did not 'get drunk or gamble' and so he formed a twice weekly club of 'hard-reading men' when they would also eat oysters, cold beef and pie.

PHWORR! THAT WAS A HARD READ ...FANCY AN OYSTER MEN?

In contrast Cochburn, a Fellow here in the mid 1800's and the most dreaded cross examining lawyer in Britain, introduced claret as port's competitor into the Fellows' Combination Room - despite being himself called after a port. This did not stop the Fellows enjoying port and in their parlour there is a half-moon table at which they can sit and enjoy it being brought to them from right to left in the traditional manner by two trucks on rails worked by a wooden lever.

Sir Herbert Jenner Fust, yet another well known lawyer and a Master of the College, argued a case on behalf of the Bishop of Exeter supporting 'unconditional baptismal regeneration' for everyone, which led to it being said that he was 'taking away from devout Christians their last hope of eternal damnation'.

Leslie Stephen, Fellow from 1854, was not afraid of eternal damnation. He had shocked people by running in a race half naked because of the heat (imagine it, a naked male torso in the 1850's) and, having taken Holy Orders, he later changed his mind and gave them up. He kept his surplice in a cupboard and every so often took it out for a good look and then kicked it back in again without regret. His contemporary Henry Fawcett, Fellow from 1856, was blinded relatively young in a shooting accident. He continued to ride, skate, fish and climb mountains (he had given up shooting) and later became Member of Parliament followed by Cabinet Minister.

People were made of less stern stuff towards the end of the 19th century as illustrated by Henry Latham, Master from 1888, who thought Cambridge was not what it used to be: 'As a seat of learning it is doomed, as a third class watering-place it has a great future.' He regretted the Old Days and used to say of one of his predecessors, Bishop Gardiner: 'He burnt one of the Fellows (for contrary religious views). Now if I were to burn the most insignificant undergraduate, I should never hear the last of it.'

UNDERGRADUATES DON'T BURN THE WAY THEY USED TO

Poor Latham had further problems. He could not

pronounce his 'r's and would tell the new students that 'here you must either wead, wide or wow' and he could not tell one woman from another, 'they are all so much alike'. Not a problem faced by Turner, bursar in the 1930's who fined a student £1 for an offence which usually carried a fine a third of that sum, 6s 8d. The student's offence was to have given his gown to his girlfriend and the bursar therefore fined him '6s 8d for not wearing your gown, 6s 8d for giving it to someone who is not a member of the University and 6s 8d for not having better taste in young women'. How humiliating!

More fortunate members of the College have included Admiral Lord Howard of Effingham, here in the 16th century and commander of the fleet which destroyed the Spanish Armada, J.B Priestley, Robert Runcie, College dean from 1956 and then Archbishop of Canterbury, Viscount Fitzwilliam of the Fitzwilliam Museum fame, Henry James who thought the Fellows' garden 'the prettiest corner of the world' and Robert 'gather ye rosebuds while ye may' Herrick, which is the Cambridge way of saying the more common 'make hay while the sun shines'.

The last word goes to Charles Darwin on his 'spell' at Cambridge:

'I cannot help looking back to these times with much pleasure...'

ACKNOWLEDGEMENTS

The History of Cambridge and of Waltham Abbey - Thomas Fuller 17th c 1940 Ed
History of the University and Colleges of Cambridge
including notes relating to the Founders and Eminent Men - G. Dyer 1814
The Story of Cambridge - C.W. Stubbs 1905
Cambridge and its Story - Arthur Gray 1912
Romance of the Cambridge Colleges - Francis Gribble 1913
Cambridge Past and Present - Brian Downs 1926
The Colleges of Cambridge - Bryan Little 1973
This College studded marsh - a humorous listing of the Cambridge Colleges - R. Kenny 1990
A History of the University of Cambridge - C. Brooke 1993
The various guides published by Jarrold Publishing and by individual colleges.
Finally, special thanks to Olivier Gazay for proof reading and constant encouragement and to
Michelle Diment for her patience in typing this dinosaur's longhand.

Richard Breen
9th May 1997

Published by
Penny Publishing Limited
London

The following section has been dedicated to some of the local guest houses, hotels, restaurants and shopkeepers who have helped to sponsor this book by kindly advertising within its pages. I hope that you will help us to repay their generosity... by paying them a visit !

ACCOMODATION

145 GWYDIR STREET
Cambridge CB1 2LJ
Tel: 01223 356615
Fax: 01223 356615
Terraced Victorian town house, close to the City Centre.

ARUNDEL HOUSE HOTEL
Chesterton Road, Cambridge CB4 3AN
Tel: 01223 367701
Fax: 01223 367721
Elegant, privately owned 105 bedroom C19th Victorian Terrace Hotel, beautifully located overlooking the River Cam and open parkland, only a few minutes walk from the City Centre and historic University Colleges, with a reputation for providing some of the best food in the area at very modest prices.

ASHLEY HOTEL
74 Chesterton Road, Cambridge CB4 3AN
Tel: 01223 350059
Small, comfortable, privately owned hotel close to the City Centre with 10 attractively furnished well equipped bedrooms. Bed and breakfast only but all the facilities of the nearby Arundel House Hotel (under same ownership) are available to Ashley Hotel residents, including a free taxi service for dinner in Arundel House Hotel's Restaurant.

BON ACCORD HOUSE
20 St Margret's Square (off Cherry Hinton Road), Cambridge CB1 4AP
Tel: 01223 411188
E-mail: bon.accord.house@dial.pipex.com
Quiet situation on good bus route. No smoking bed & breakfast accommodation.

CARLTON LODGE
245 Chesterton Road, Cambridge CB4 1AS
Tel: 01223 367792
Fax: 01223 566877
E-mail: carlton_lodge@psilink.co.uk
Centrally located guest house with own off-road parking. All rooms have T.V., tea and coffee making facilities and central heating.

CHRISTINA'S GUEST HOUSE
47 St Andrew's Road, Cambridge CB4 1DH
Tel: 01223 365855 / 327700
Fax: 01223 365855
Guests are assured of a warm welcome here, quietly located in the beautiful City of Cambridge, only 15 minutes walk from the City Centre and Colleges. All rooms have colour T.V. and tea/coffee making equipment. Some rooms have private shower and toilet. Centrally heated with comfortable T.V. lounge. Private car park, locked at night ETB COMMENDED. RAC ACCLAIMED. AA RECOMMENDED QQQ

HELEN HOTEL
167-169 Hills Road, Cambridge CB2 2RJ
Tel: 01223 246465
Fax: 01223 214406
Comfort with a personal and friendly welcome. All bedrooms are en-suite, tea/coffee making facilities, T.V., telephone and hair dryer.

MR & MRS SCHUSTER BEESLEY
56 St. Barnabas Road, Cambridge CB1 2DE
Tel: 01223 350543
B&B. Central Cambridge. Quiet twin or double room. Private facilities. T.V. Tea & coffee. No smoking. Parking available. Open all year.

PANOS HOTEL & RESTAURANT
154-156 Hills Road, Cambridge CB2 2PB
Tel: 01223 212958
Fax: 01223 210980
Opened in 1979 by Genevieve Kretz, who is French, and her Greek Cypriot husband, The Panos serves only top quality French and Greek cuisine, all cooked to order, and offers very comfortable and well appointed hotel bedrooms.

REGENCY GUEST HOUSE
7 Regent Terrace, Cambridge CB2 1AA
Tel: 01223 329626
Fax: 01223 301567
Friendly, comfortable Victorian house in the centre of Cambridge.
Offering high standards of accommodation overlooking City Park known as
Parkers' Piece!

SOUTHAMPTON HOUSE
7 Elizabeth Way, Cambridge CB4 1DE
Tel: 01223 357780
Fax: 01223 314297
ETB COMMENDED. AA RECOMMENDED QQQ. PARKING

TUDOR COTTAGE BED & BREAKFAST
292 Histon Road, Cambridge CB4 3HS
TEL: 01223 565212
FAX: 01223 565660
Comfortable en-suite room with T.V. tea/coffee facilities in friendly family house.
Parking.

RESTAURANTS

ARUNDEL HOUSE HOTEL
Chesterton Road, Cambridge CB4 3AN
Tel: 01223 367701
Fax: 01223 367721
Arundel House Hotel's Restaurant has achieved a reputation for providing some of the best food in the area and yet it is not expensive. (AA Rosette and RAC Restaurant Awards amongst its many accolades) Wide range of dishes on Table d'hôte and A la carte menus together with separate vegetarian and children's menus. Also all day menu in Victorian style conservatory. TDH lunch 3 course £10.95, 2 course £9.75 Dinner £15.95 Conservatory dishes £2.45 - £6.75.

CAFFÉ UNO
32 Bridge Street, Cambridge
Tel: 01223 314 954
In the heart of Cambridge, by the riverside, lies an Italian restaurant of unquestionable good taste. Its name: Caffé Uno!

PANOS HOTEL & RESTAURANT
154-156 Hills Road, Cambridge CB2 2PB
Tel: 01223 212 958
Fax: 01223 210 980
Opened in 1979 by Genevieve Kretz, who is French, and her Greek Cypriot husband, The Panos serves only top quality French and Greek cuisine, all cooked to order, and offers very comfortable and well appointed hotel bedrooms.

SHOPPING

THE ORGANISER SHOP
40 Green Street, Cambridge CB2 3JX
TEL: 01223 361212
FAX: 01223 234045
Comprehensive range of organisers, diaries, writing instruments. Leather goods and gifts available at all price points. 10% off full R.R.P. on production of this book!

If you have enjoyed
CAMBRIDGE - ODDFELLOWS & FUNNY TALES
Then you're going to love

TO ORDER:
TELEPHONE 0171 720 1166
OR SEND A CHEQUE FOR £4.99
PLUS £1 P&P (UK)
MADE PAYABLE TO:

PENNY PUBLISHING LIMITED
218A STEWART'S COURT, STEWART'S ROAD
LONDON SW8 4UB
TEL 0171 720 1166 FAX 0171 720 1177
E-mail: pennygroup@btinternet.com